T0328780

Cambridge Elements ≡

Elements in Public and Nonprofit Administration
edited by
Andrew Whitford
University of Georgia
Robert Christensen
Brigham Young University

CONTINGENT COLLABORATION

When to Use Which Models for Joined-up Government

Rodney J. Scott
University of New South Wales
Eleanor R. K. Merton

CAMBRIDGE
UNIVERSITY PRESS

University Printing House, Cambridge CB2 8BS, United Kingdom

One Liberty Plaza, 20th Floor, New York, NY 10006, USA

477 Williamstown Road, Port Melbourne, VIC 3207, Australia

314–321, 3rd Floor, Plot 3, Splendor Forum, Jasola District Centre, New Delhi – 110025, India

103 Penang Road, #05–06/07, Visioncrest Commercial, Singapore 238467

Cambridge University Press is part of the University of Cambridge.

It furthers the University's mission by disseminating knowledge in the pursuit of education, learning, and research at the highest international levels of excellence.

www.cambridge.org
Information on this title: www.cambridge.org/9781009124454
DOI: 10.1017/9781009128513

First published 2022

A catalogue record for this publication is available from the British Library.

ISBN 978-1-009-12445-4 Paperback
ISSN 2515-4303 (online)
ISSN 2515-429X (print)

Cambridge University Press has no responsibility for the persistence or accuracy of URLs for external or third-party internet websites referred to in this publication and does not guarantee that any content on such websites is, or will remain, accurate or appropriate.

Contingent Collaboration

When to Use Which Models for Joined-up Government

Elements in Public and Nonprofit Administration

DOI: 10.1017/9781009128513
First published online: June 2022

Rodney J. Scott
University of New South Wales
Eleanor R. K. Merton

Author for correspondence: Rodney J. Scott, rodney.scott@gmail.com

Abstract: The question of how agencies can work together has been central to the field of public administration for several decades. Despite significant research, the process of collaboration can still be a fraught endeavour for practitioners. Nevertheless, agencies keep trying to work together because it is the only way to make progress on the biggest challenges facing public administrators. This Element reveals the deeply contingent nature of collaboration, rejecting the idea that collaboration can be reduced to a universal best practice. The New Zealand government has implemented such a contingent approach that maps different collaborative methods against problem settings and the degree of trade-off required from the actors' core or individual work. This Element provides a detailed case study of the New Zealand approach, and eighteen embedded elements or 'model' collaborative forms for joined-up government. It explains how New Zealand public servants approach the important question: 'When to use which models?'

This Element also has a video abstract: www.cambridge.org/scott-merton

Keywords: collaboration, contingency, joined-up government, public administration, New Zealand

ISBNs: 9781009124454 (PB), 9781009128513 (OC)
ISSNs: 2515-4303 (online), 2515-429X (print)

Contents

1 The Necessity of Interagency Collaboration

This is the hardest challenge there is; when agency goals compete with collective goals, agency goals almost always win.

(Lewis Holden, Chief Executive, Ministry for Culture and Heritage)

The question of how the component parts of government should organize themselves has long been central to the field of public administration. Governments around the world have found it necessary to divide up their administrations into smaller units with more manageable scopes, allowing problems to be assigned wholly to one of the disaggregated agencies. Such specialization along organizational divisions of labour has been hailed as an 'engine of value creation', having its roots in the first streams of organizational theory (March and Simon 1958; Bardach 1998).

Divisions between agencies proved effective in addressing some issues. In the 1980s and 1990s, many jurisdictions implemented a range of reforms that later became known as 'New Public Management' (NPM), adding strong vertical hierarchies to narrow-focus agencies, reinforced by accountability systems and incentives. The reforms were influenced by neoliberal market theory and were intended to address fiscal pressures produced by various financial crises (Scott 2001). Broadly speaking, these reforms achieved their intended efficiency gains but also brought some unintended consequences and exacerbated other existing challenges. The interaction of strong vertical lines of accountability and highly specialized agencies encouraged the proliferation of 'siloed' working, a term that will be familiar for its now ubiquitous derision from both inside and outside government. While collaboration has never been easy, years of emphasizing vertical hierarchies have left many governments ill-equipped to work horizontally (Boston et al. 1996). Collaboration must be 'retrofitted' into an NPM system that did not inherently encourage it (Eppel and O'Leary 2021, p. 1).

In the complex, volatile world of the twenty-first century, the most persistent problems facing public administrators span agency boundaries (O'Leary 2014). In part, this is the result of past successes – more progress has been made on those problems that could be addressed effectively by agencies working in siloes. Consequently, the most pressing problems that remain tend to be the ones that span agency boundaries. Elsewhere, it is the result of past failures – some problems that governments thought could be solved in siloes have proven resistant to policy intervention, and governments now realize that making progress on these less-tractable problems requires agencies to work together. Other drivers and factors such as heightened interdependency and uncertainty (Thomson 2001; Thomson and Perry 2006; Emerson et al. 2012) feed into the increased interest in and necessity of collaboration. Bardach (1998) suggests that systemic features of public management indicate abundant opportunities to create public value through collaboration, by both increasing performance and reducing costs. Working together provides more levers for solving problems and access to more resources (Krueger 2005). Thus, work that spans agency boundaries has emerged as the 'new normal' for public servants (Carey and Harris 2016, p. 112).

Yet, for a variety of reasons, collaboration is a fraught and frequently costly endeavour (Sullivan et al. 2012). Interagency collaboration consists of ongoing negotiation, which has significant coordination costs compared to the efficiency of a simple hierarchy (Van Huyck et al. 1990). Without hierarchy, decision-making requires time-consuming consensus building in order to be supported overall (Ren et al. 2005). Imperfect alignment of collaborative goals may introduce the risk of some parties opportunistically pursuing their individual goals (Laan et al. 2011). Even when collaboration is successful, the transaction costs tend to be very high (Scott and Boyd 2020). Interagency collaboration has accordingly been referred to in the field of public administration as both the 'philosopher's stone' (Jennings and Krane 1994) and 'holy grail' (Peters 1998).

1.1 Contribution of This Element

Interagency collaboration has attracted significant attention in public adminis-tration literature; indeed, questions of how to collaborate effectively are the 'most discussed questions involved in the performance of public institutions and the achievement of public purpose' (Kettl and Kelman 2007, p. 45). We were therefore sceptical that the field needed another book on this topic, one that would revisit many of the same observations and arguments. However, this Element is intended as something a little different – focusing not on how to do interagency collaboration but instead on exploring when public servants employ different approaches, arrangements, or models to address different problem contexts. We wrote it because of a recognition that the treatment of interagency collaboration is lacking – many researchers continue to seek, and report on, the success factors that will make collaboration easy, without speci-fying how such factors are reliant on context (a limitation observed by O'Toole and Meier 2004, Chen 2010, Sedgwick 2017, and Prentice et al. 2019).

The first significant contribution of this Element is in reconceptualizing the field of collaboration as a set of contingent responses applied to specific contexts. Carey and Crammond's (2015) evidence synthesis explored the ques-tion of 'what works' in interagency collaboration and found scant overlap except at the broadest levels. Instead, as observed by Prentice et al. (2019), best practice requires a deliberate deployment of different collaborative arrangements to solve equally different problems. The specific focus on contingency – applying different solutions to different problems and problem settings – sets this Element apart from other research in the discipline to provide an example of how one jurisdiction answers the sorely neglected question of when different collaborative models should be used.

While few authors explicitly claim that their findings represent a single universal best practice, it is an implicit part of identifying generalizable success factors for interagency collaboration. This is a trap into which even the authors of this Element have fallen in the past, reporting that collaborative success could be supported by focusing on a small number of problems, setting measurable targets, and assigning shared responsibility to a few senior leaders (Scott and Bardach 2019; Scott and Boyd 2020; Scott and Merton 2021). Across a similar period, another group of New Zealand researchers studied different collaborative case studies and concluded that what was needed was a 'guardian angel', 'entrepreneur', and 'fellow travellers' (Eppel et al. 2014). Neither group delineated where and when their unique findings might apply.

The contention that collaborative approaches should be contingent echoes developments in the broader field of management. 'Scientific' management pursued universal best practice (Taylor 2004), and when universality proved elusive, the field became increasingly interested in the ways that good management practices differed depending on context (Woodward 1965). Similar developments can be observed in public administration, where simple and universal solutions have gradually been replaced with more nuanced and contingent solutions (see examples later in this section).

Some ground has been broken on a contingent approach to interagency collaboration (Lee and Scott 2019), with calls for a 'collaborative toolbox' or 'dimensional approach to collaboration', in which different collaborative practices are indicated by different contextual factors (Prentice et al. 2019, p. 792). This Element goes even further to directly address the core question raised by O'Toole and Meier (2004), Chen (2010), Sedgwick (2017), Lee and Scott (2019), and Prentice et al. (2019) – given the variety of possible collaboration arrangements, when should each be used?

This contribution should not, however, be overstated. While the Element presents a contingent approach to collaboration within the New Zealand central government, it is also limited by that context. It cannot answer the question of whether such arrangements would respond effectively to central government collaboration in other jurisdictions, to local government, or to cross-sectoral collaboration. Nonetheless, it provides an example of a contingent approach in action that may inspire similar approaches elsewhere, potentially with a different set of contingencies.

This Element's second area of contribution is to fill a methodological niche in the study of interagency collaboration. The key point of departure is in the unit of analysis. Literature on collaboration often reports detailed findings from individual case studies (e.g., Walter and Petr 2000; Darlington et al. 2005; Noonan et al. 2008), or from comparisons of cases deemed similar for the purpose of reporting commonality of structures and tools, politics, and craft (e.g., Bardach 1998; Bogdanor 2005; Peters 2015; Agranoff 2017). Periodically, when the findings of collaborative governance literature become too disorganized and contradictory, authors will conduct a meta-analysis or evidence synthesis, reporting common themes that often become vague or anodyne (e.g., McGuire 2006; Carey and Crammond 2015) as they seek to draw out commonality from what we argue are different solutions to different problems.

These methodologies gloss over the diversity of collaborative arrangements and their problem contexts and result in a failure to map different problems with their best corresponding collaborative solutions. Several authors have noted that this is an area where 'collaborative practice is ahead of scholarship' (Prentice et al. 2019, p. 792; similar sentiments in McGuire 2002; Bryson et al. 2015; Lee and Scott 2019). This Element, therefore, explores the topic both as a theoretical exercise and as an integrated case study of a single jurisdiction – New Zealand. Doing so allows for a more detailed examination of the internal logic and elements embedded in one government's coherent system of interagency collaboration. We argue that it is primarily the logic of this contingent framework that is interesting and have not evaluated whether the presence of such a framework has improved performance, though we note a positive reception by those public servants who use it.

The third contribution made by this Element is in documenting practices in a jurisdiction of high international interest. New Zealand has occupied this position of interest in public administration for several decades, having moved further and faster than other nations in implementing the NPM reforms of the 1980s (Pallott 1999). The reforms resulted in a highly efficient but fragmented system not easily able to address problems that fall outside single-agency remits (Boston et al. 1996). New Zealand's public service is regularly considered high performing (Halligan 2004), with a history of reflective practice that actively engages with public administration theory (Donadelli and Lodge 2019; Scott et al. 2022). It continues to be highly regarded as a leader in administrative practice (Craft and Halligan 2020; Scott et al. 2020).

Despite this reputation for high performance, many authors note that the New Zealand public service has occasionally struggled to collaborate effectively (Eppel et al. 2014; O'Leary 2014), operating more as a constellation of independent actors rather than a coherent whole (Jensen et al. 2014). In this context, the collaborative practices described in this Element represent a response to a perceived weakness or challenge. We cannot claim that the collaborative practices used in New Zealand are the most successful, or even that the dimensions for differentiating a contingent approach are the most salient. Such claims could require much greater testing, replication, and rigorous analysis. Nor can we claim that New Zealand practices are fully generalizable – at the very least, key features like a unitary (not federal) and parliamentary system of government will make a difference. Instead, we present the case study as an example of contingency-in-action, identifying the ways in which one nation is contending with the multitude of problems that require collaborative solutions.

1.2 Defining Interagency Collaboration

The vast body of collaboration literature offers a variety of overlapping and conflicting language and definitions for describing similar practices. In this text, we use the term 'interagency collaboration' to refer broadly to agencies working together to achieve a specific purpose. However, we also explore how similar language is used elsewhere, locating this text within its disciplinary context.

In the most general sense, interagency collaboration refers to a range of practices that involve agencies working together (Axelsson and Axelsson 2006). Bardach also offers an inclusive definition of collaboration as 'any joint activity by two or more agencies that is intended to increase public value by their working together rather than separately' (1998, p. 8). However, some authors use the term more specifically, differentiating it from other modes of interagency working such as 'cooperation' or 'coordination' (e.g., Marrett 1971; Gregson et al. 1992; Huxham and Macdonald 1992; Gajda 2004; Sadoff and Grey 2005; Thomson and Perry 2006; Horwath and Morrison 2007; Keast et al. 2007; Eppel et al. 2014). Many of these same authors consider coordination, cooperation, and collaboration as part of a spectrum of interagency working, usually from 'distant' to 'close', and where closer collaboration is more difficult and often requires shared history to execute effectively (Marrett 1971; Huxham and Macdonald 1992; Brown and Keast 2003; Gajda 2004).

For example, Gray (1989) suggests that collaboration takes place over a longer period, while cooperation and coordination are sometimes its precursors, taking place over shorter periods. Keast et al. (2007) similarly see cooperation and coordination as an earlier stage of a more distant connection, involving information-sharing and planning together, while collaboration takes the next step into actually performing actions together. Eppel et al. (2014) add that collaboration corresponds to shared responsibility, while cooperation and coordination would at most involve common interests. The conception of collaboration as a spectrum is supported by evidence that relationships mature, and trust is built as agreements are reached, conflicts resolved, and commitments delivered (Ostrom 1998; Huxham and Vangen 2000; Koppenjan and Klijn 2004; Ansell and Gash 2008). In summation, Thomson and Perry's survey of the literature concludes that collaboration can only be defined in contrast with cooperation and coordination, as involving deeper 'interaction, integration, commitment and complexity' (2006, p. 23). This text borrows the concept of a spectrum, but goes further in suggesting that some types of interagency work are more appropriate in different contexts; different forms of interagency work do not simply differ in their complexity but are more suitable for responding to different problems.

1.2.1 Collaborative Governance, Network Governance, and Joined-Up Government

This text is primarily concerned with how government agencies can collaborate effectively in different contexts. These processes and functions can be broadly grouped as 'governance', defined by Bevir (2012) as the processes of interaction of an organized society over a social system. Thus, how government agencies can collaborate could be described as 'collaborative governance', though this phrase has been used elsewhere with a specific meaning.

Ansell and Gash (2008), having identified wide-ranging use of terminology as a barrier to theory building, define the term 'collaborative governance' restrictively, stressing the inclusion of non-state actors, whether non-governmental organizations (NGOs), business representatives, community leaders, stakeholder groups, or other individual members of civil society. In contrast, Emerson et al. (2012) take a broader view, defining the term to include decision-making processes and structures between any collaborating parties

Collaborative governance between government agencies differs from collaborative governance in the private sector due to difficulty in attribution of social outcomes (Thompson 2014), complex authorizing environments, and different motivations of public servants (e.g., 'public service motivation', Perry and Hondeghem 2008; and 'mission valence', Wright and Pandey 2011). Collaboration between government agencies also differs from collaboration involving non-governmental organizations, in that the mechanisms for political control are different, and much of the literature on inter-sectoral collaboration emphasizes capacity and capability gaps in non-governmental organizations that are less common in large, well-resourced government agencies (Kania and Kramer 2011). Government agencies usually lack the freedom to choose which other agencies they would like to collaborate with, and when; if two or more agencies don't have good relationships, they are stuck trying to make an unhappy partnership work regardless (Scott and Bardach 2019). Though not always the case, collaboration in and with other sectors can seek to capitalize on momentary alignment, opportunity, and collaborative 'windows' (Takahashi and Smutny 2002).

Interagency collaboration can also be distinguished from the literature on 'networks', in that the formal accountabilities of government agencies differ from the looser goal alignment seen in network literature (Jones et al. 1997; Provan and Milward 2001; Keast et al. 2006; Provan and Kenis 2008; Sørensen and Torfing 2016). However, loose and informal networks characterize several of the models in this Element, so the boundary is not absolute.

'Joined-up government' is a more recent term to describe collaboration between government agencies, used in an equally mixed body of literature. The term is commonly associated with the UK government under Prime Minister Tony Blair and describes a government that is able to overcome its internal barriers (Bogdanor 2005). Joined-up government is sometimes conceived of as a seamless service experience across multiple agencies (Davies 2009) and sometimes refers more broadly to processes that take a holistic approach to addressing complex policy problems (Carey and Harris 2016; Scott and Boyd 2016).

Ultimately, 'interagency collaboration' seemed like the least-bad terminology to describe the activities discussed in this Element. The topic (and related fields) would benefit from greater definitional and categorical clarity, but that is beyond the scope of this text. Both Bingham and O'Leary (2006) and Getha-Taylor et al. (2019) find collaboration research guilty of 'parallel play', where researchers in different disciplines are working independently on related problems, but not paying attention to each other's work. In choosing the term interagency collaboration, we still intend that the discussion be informed by related fields and that interagency collaboration be informed by collaboration in other contexts while acknowledging some limits to transferability.

1.2.2 Describing and Analyzing Collaboration

Such semantic exercises and debates, although common in the body of collaboration literature, are of limited use when it comes to actually understanding the mechanics of collaboration. Despite enormous attention in public administration literature, collaboration remains a 'fraught' endeavour (Sullivan et al. 2012, p. 41) that is often unable to demonstrate 'collaborative advantage' (Huxham and Vangen 2013, p. 1; Doberstein 2016, p. 819). Beyond failing to deliver results, collaboration is expensive, involving high opportunity and transaction costs (Van Huyck et al. 1990; Bardach 2001; Krueger 2005; Head 2013). This is generally observed to be true of all forms of collaboration, and specifically true of interagency collaboration (Davies 2009; Kwon and Feiock 2010). Such costs are usually present in consensus/inclusive decision-making due to inefficiency and include time and effort, as well as the impacts of distrust or frustration (Ren et al. 2005; Doberstein 2016; Scott and Bardach 2019; Waardenburg et al. 2020). Difficulties associated with collaboration also arise from inadequate practices for determining attribution (Thompson 2014) and assigning accountability (Page 2004). Collaboration, the literature reveals, 'is like cottage cheese; it occasionally smells bad and separates easily' (Thomson and Perry 1998, p. 409).

There was a time when collaborative practice was a 'black box' (Thomson and Perry 2006, p. 20), but there have now been dozens of studies that attempt to shine a light on how public administrators go about collaborating (Diaz-Kope et al. 2015). Thomson and Perry (2006) and Chen (2010) each propose a simple model for understanding collaborative success (and failure), in which 'contextual factors' interact with collaborative 'processes and functions' to produce a range of outcomes. These can be conceived of as the independent, moderating, and dependent variables (respectively) of collaborative effectiveness (see Figure 1). The contextual category absorbs a range of factors referred to in the literature variously as antecedents, drivers, starting conditions, environmental constraints, history, and needs. Processes and functions include consideration of goals, relationship with political principals, incentives, and funding and resourcing. The desired outcomes can be in the form of public value or assessed through proxy measures for effective collaborative processes and behaviours.

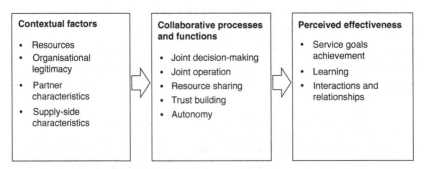

Figure 1 Examples of independent, moderating, and dependent variables in collaborative effectiveness

O'Leary and Vij (2012, p. 516) outline the need to identify a 'comprehensive vision of the antecedents, processes, and outcomes' as a major research challenge for collaboration literature, however, each remains contested. Various authors consider contextual factors in different ways. Some limit their observations to collaboration in a particular context – for example, Prentice et al. (2019) provide a lengthy list of collaboration studies in different policy settings. Others consider the public administration settings in which collaboration is attempted (Eppel and O'Leary 2021). Some authors limit their observations to collaboration between different categories of collaborative partners; for example, Bardach (1998) describes interagency collaboration, Agranoff (2017) describes collaboration between government jurisdictions, and Ansell and Gash (2008) describe collaboration between government and non-government organizations. Others distinguish between collaboration that arises from the top-down versus bottom-up (Chen 2010), or explore the contextual conditions that explain why people want to collaborate (Diaz-Kope and Morris 2019). Donahue (2004) offers a framework for categorizing collaborative contexts across a variety of dimensions: formality, duration, focus (broad versus narrow), institutional diversity (types of actors), number of actors, stability, initiation (by which actors), and problem versus opportunity-driven.

Some studies focus on specific aspects of collaborative processes in trying to understand why some collaborations succeed and others fail. Osborne and Gaebler (1992) conceive of collaboration almost exclusively through formal reorganization, while Bardach specifically excludes structural elements to focus on behaviours and processes (1998). Others describe 'multidimensional frameworks' for collaborative processes (Agranoff and McGuire 2003; Imperial 2005; Thomson and Perry 2006; Bowman and Parsons 2013; Prentice et al. 2019). For example, Thomson and Perry (2006) break collaboration down into five dimensions: governance, administration, mutuality, norms, and organizational autonomy. Prentice et al. (2019) describe eleven 'collaborative tools' under the categories of structure, governance, and commitment. Several notable texts (McGuire 2002; Ansell and Gash 2008; Bryson et al. 2015) further explore dimensional approaches in the context of network governance, collaborative governance, and cross-sectoral collaboration, respectively.

Even the desired outcomes of collaboration are contested (Carey and Harris 2016; Scott and Boyd 2016), with different possible parameters for determining effectiveness (see Marsh and McConnell 2010 for a broader discussion of 'success' in a public administration context). Delays between cause and effect (Carey and Harris 2016), and difficulty in assigning attribution (Thompson 2014), have caused some authors to argue for the use of process measures to determine whether parties are demonstrating collaborative behaviours.

Others compare collaborative behaviours to 'collaboration theatre' (Scott and Boyd 2016, p. 238) where much activity results in little of value, and argue instead for a focus on 'intermediate outcomes' that balance intrinsic value with attribution and delay (Scott and Boyd 2017, p. 4). In another text in this series, Getha-Taylor (2019) explores the sustainability of collaboration as an important outcome in some contexts.

The literature now includes extensive separate descriptions of contexts, processes, and outcomes. While collaboration is no longer the 'black box' it once was, results are still mixed (Thomson and Perry 2006). Several authors have suggested that this is because collaboration is not one thing (O'Toole and Meier 2004; Chen 2010; Sedgwick 2017; Lee and Scott 2019; Prentice et al. 2019) – there are many different contexts for collaboration, and different processes and functions will be more effective in each context. Like these authors, we contend that continued searches for best-practice approaches to collaboration are likely to yield limited results.

1.2.3 Social Antecedents to Collaboration

While public administration theory has 'long emphasised the distinctive character and motives associated with public institutions' (Perry 1997, p. 181), the past two decades have seen increased attention paid to psychological, behavioural, and social dimensions of public service. Constructs like public service motivation, mission valence, goal commitment, social identity, and interpersonal trust are acknowledged as important predictors of public servant behaviour and contribute to public outcomes (Scott 2019).

Public servants have a range of motivations, including a belief in the value of public institutions and a desire to achieve positive social change (Perry 1996). Public service motivation is enhanced by alignment between the values of the individual and the goals of the agency ('mission valence', Wright and Pandey 2011), or in this case, the goals of the collaborative activity. This is related to 'goal commitment', which refers to the volitional bond between public servants and achievement of the collaborative goal (Locke et al. 1988). Even the most successful collaborations are not without pain, cost, and frustration; in these situations, collaboration is sometimes sustained over time and able to overcome setbacks when the participants were strongly committed to the goal (Scott and Merton 2021; Scott and Boyd 2022).

Collaboration is easier between people who feel like they are on the same team, with more resource sharing and charity concern (Brewer and Hewstone 2004; Scott 2019). 'Social identity' refers to the branch of psychology that concerns individuals' conceptions of themselves as members of groups

(Tajfel 1974). Absent that sense of teamwork, the next best option appears to be trusting relationships between collaborative partners on different teams (Tschannen-Moran 2001; Vangen and Huxham 2003; Hattori and Lapidus 2004). However, more recent literature has begun to explore how collaboration can be sustained in the absence of trust (Getha-Taylor et al. 2019). Getha-Taylor et al. define collaborative trust as 'an individual perception that is the product of one's assessments, experiences, and dispositions, in which one believes, and is willing to act on, the words, actions, and decisions of others' (p. 60). They make the important observation that collaboration can succeed (albeit with potentially higher monitoring costs) in the absence of interpersonal trust, if there is trust in the 'principles, rules, norms, and decision-making procedures' (p. 60).

Finally, we consider 'collaborative capacity' (Bardach 2001, p. 21), the combination of interpersonal skills that public servants bring to the task of collaborating. Whether this 'craft' (Bardach 2001, p. 3) is innate or can be learned through teaching or experience, is still up for debate. However, O'Leary (2014) suggested that collaborative capacity was not a competency that was universally held by senior New Zealand public servants. O'Leary called for an investment in collaborative capacity and training to support 'new ways of leading in a world of shared problems' (p. 50).

We interpret the aforementioned psychological, behavioural, and social factors as generally favourable to collaboration. Although we have not seen such a claim made directly, perhaps authors in favour of a collaborative capacity approach believe such an approach will obviate the need for an ex ante contingent framework. Capable collaborators will perhaps be able to navigate, innovate and adapt collaborative approaches in response to their emerging and dynamic context. While difficult to establish empirically, we consider it plausible that collaborative success is supported by a mix of general and adaptive collaborative capacity, and specific contingent socio-technical features.

1.3 The Argument for a Contingent Approach

Many studies on collaboration describe some aspects of context and process (see, e.g., Bardach 2001; Thomson and Perry 2006; Ansell and Gash 2008; Emerson et al. 2012; Bryson et al. 2015; Carey and Crammond 2015). Combined with the many studies that discuss a spectrum of solutions (from cooperation to coordination to collaboration), collaboration literature now separately explores different contexts and different processes and functions, without combining these aspects into a framework for matching problems with solutions.

This problem – emerging acknowledgement of different problems and different solutions, but without means to match the two – is most obvious in edited volumes. For example, O'Flynn et al. (2013) include separately authored case studies from around the world. In an introductory chapter, O'Flynn observes that 'determining what works and in what circumstances is part of the challenge for scholars and policy-makers' (2013, p. 6). The chapters that follow each report different success factors without making links to other chapters, and without indication of which success factors correspond to which contexts. The best a practitioner can do on reading such a text is to conclude 'perhaps my problem looks most like those considered in Chapter x' and then draw on the success factors described in that chapter.

In this Element, we join with a growing number of authors (like O'Flynn mentioned earlier) who call for a more contingent approach (see also, O'Toole and Meier 2004; Chen 2010; Sedgwick 2017; Lee and Scott 2019; Prentice et al. 2019). A contingent approach simply describes the discretionary application of management solutions to meet specific contexts (Fiedler 1993). We echo Prentice et al. (2019, p. 803) who claim, 'researchers' inability to uncover and comprehend these contingencies is the principal reason that collaboration scholarship lags practice'. The field of network management has made some progress in understanding management contingencies (see, e.g., Verweij et al. 2013; Hovik and Hanssen 2015; Cristofoli et al. 2019); however, the dynamics described appear significantly different to those reported in the more structured world of interagency collaboration.

Contingency theories were developed in the 1950s and 1960s as a reaction to perceived limitations with Taylor's scientific theory of management (2004), which suggested a single best way to manage an organization. Tannenbaum and Schmidt (1957) developed a leadership continuum (analogous to the cooperation–coordination–collaboration continuum discussed earlier) based on levels of functional autonomy for subordinate workers. Fiedler's 'Contingency Model' (1964) proposed a direct relationship between a management context and the appropriate management style. At the same time, Blake and Mouton developed their 'Managerial Grid Model' (1964), that mapped management styles against a dimension model of 'concern for people' and 'concern for production'. Hersey and Blanchard promoted a similar dimensional framework in their 'Situational Leadership Theory' (1969). In each case, management researchers in the 1950s and 60s were beginning to take a more discriminatory approach to matching problems with solutions, abandoning the quest for single universal best practice.

In this text, we group all these approaches ('contingency', 'grid', and 'situational') under the broad heading of 'contingent' or 'contingency' approaches.

We refer to the mapping of problems to solutions using a categorical grid as a 'dimensional' approach following usage in the psychological literature (Hayes et al. 1996) and applied it to collaboration by Prentice et al. (2019).

1.3.1 Contingency Theory in Public Administration

This is not the first time that contingency approaches have been applied in public administration literature. Like many applied academic fields, public administration literature is filled with frameworks for describing and classifying observations. For example, in writing about NPM reforms, Dunleavy and Hood (1994) apply a simple two-by-two grid (degree of generalized rules, degree of separation of public and private spheres) based on 'grid group cultural theory' (Douglas 1982). Peters and Pierre (1998) map six case studies against dimensions of NPM (limited, intermediate, extensive) and 'governance' (limited, extensive). Hood (2000) maps 'public service bargains' on a grid with 'cost to politicians' on the vertical axis (with four values), and the type of agency bargain on the horizontal axis (with three values, producing twelve named public service bargains). These and countless other examples present categories in a grid or dimensional format but are not contingent approaches because they are purely descriptive and do not match solutions to problem types.

However, the literature also abounds in prescriptive frameworks that are explicitly contingent, following an 'if/then' operational logic (though not, pertinent to this Element, for describing interagency collaboration). Greenwood et al. (1975) and Hinings et al. (1975) apply contingency theory to local authorities, mapping contextual information (size of local authority, socioeconomic structure of constituents) to organizational structure. Williamson's discriminatory matching theory (1979) compares instruments and performance attributes as dimensions in order to prescribe hierarchical or market-based solutions to performance management. Wilson's production/procedure dimensional framework (1989) describes a contingent approach to organizational design in response to operating context. Explicitly contingent approaches have also been applied more recently to describe public administration responses to (for example): co-production with public service clients (Alford 2002), performance management (Christensen and Yoshimi 2003), accountability arrangements (Mansbridge 2014), diversity management (McGrandle 2017), and shared service centres (Elston and Dixon 2020).

We suggest that contingency theory is becoming more prevalent in public administration literature because public administration is an applied management field that has among its aims not just to describe public administration, but to inform improvements in the quality of public administration practices.

Contingency is what public administrators need – answers to the question: 'What action should I take in response to the situation I now face?' or 'When should I use which models for joined-up government?'

2 The Contingent Collaboration Toolkit

The question isn't 'what works?', it's 'what works, when?'
(Andrew Burns, Deputy Public Service Commissioner)

This Element is primarily a single-country case study, albeit one with many embedded elements. In the New Zealand central government, public servants use an explicitly contingent and dimensional framework to determine when to use which methods for interagency collaboration. As observed earlier, many scholars in the field have noted that collaboration practice is ahead of, or more advanced than, the corresponding literature. This Element aims to address this gap by documenting the advanced and discerning practices by experienced practitioners. Further, it continues a long tradition of collaborative theory being advanced by practitioner-academics (Agranoff 2017).

The New Zealand public service developed and adopted a 'Toolkit for Shared Problems' (2018, henceforth 'the Toolkit'): a two-dimensional framework that offers fifteen different collaborative methods based on different problem contexts (the Toolkit describes eighteen models, but only fifteen include collaborative arrangements). The Toolkit was developed in 2017, based on a stocktake of New Zealand's experiences with interagency collaboration in the period 2004–17. Initially, the Toolkit was an ex post framing of New Zealand experiences, but then became an ex ante tool for the design and implementation of interagency collaborative arrangements from 2017 until the time of writing in 2022. The Toolkit was revised in 2020 based on feedback from the first three years of implementation as a design tool. We therefore conceive of this study in two methodological stages:

1. How a group of public servants distilled lessons from New Zealand's experience with interagency collaboration to develop a contingent Toolkit (documented through much of this section).
2. How the authors of this Element in turn draw lessons from the case study.

With respect to the latter, the New Zealand case study described in this Element is primarily ethnographic (and partially auto-ethnographic), based on the first author's participation. Rodney Scott is a researcher from the University of New South Wales and also Chief Policy Advisor for the Public Service Commission. He was the lead advisor on the Toolkit, working closely with a group of senior public servants. While this Element is written in the former capacity, and the views expressed do not represent the Public Service Commission or the New Zealand government, the underlying study benefits from an insider's perspective. The Element draws on participant–observer field notes from during the formation of the Toolkit; government documents; and ninety-four interviews with public service leaders and stakeholders (see Appendix 1).

2.1 Public Administration in New Zealand

The New Zealand public service has long been of international interest. In part, this is due to the dramatic NPM reforms of the late 1980s (Boston et al. 1996); while reforms across the world during this period were grouped as NPM, New Zealand was characterized as going fastest and furthest (Pollitt and Bouckaert 2011). The interaction between practice and scholarship that has characterized public service reform in New Zealand also contributes; while in many parts of the world, public administration literature is left to make theoretical sense of pragmatic or politically inspired reforms, New Zealand's approach to public administration is characterized as theoretically coherent and academically pure (Lodge and Gill 2011). This was noteworthy in the interviews for this Element, where several interviewees referenced key scholarly texts in their responses.

Another explanation for international interest in the New Zealand government is that it tends to work fairly well. New Zealand scores highly on international measures of government effectiveness (Blavatnik School of Government 2019; OECD 2021), despite a much lower per-capita spend than its key comparators (OECD 2021). But that is not to say that the New Zealand government collaborates effectively – major reviews of the New Zealand public service identify fragmentation as the biggest challenge (State Services Commission 2001, 2011, The Treasury 2006)Review of the Centre 2001, 2004; State Services Commission, 2011). While Boston et al. (1996), and Gregory (2006) blame this on New Zealand's enthusiasm for single-point accountability at the expense of shared goals, O'Leary identifies a system that is so lean that managers spend all day 'playing tennis at the net' without time to collaborate, alongside a discomfort with risk, and the stifling of bottom-up innovation (2014, p. 41). The models described in this Element reflect New Zealand's preoccupation with management accountability – even 'horizontal' management is often described in terms of vertical hierarchies (Scott and Boyd 2020; Scott and Merton 2020), the only difference is that these hierarchies involve collectives – a board of chief executives dictating to a group of deputies and so on down the chain. Therefore, we have in this case study a jurisdiction known for generally performing well, but that has struggled with collaboration and tends to seek structured solutions at the top (Eppel and O'Leary 2021), even as lower-level public servants seek to work more organically and orient themselves around a sense of mission (Eppel et al. 2014).

For this study, New Zealand is also of interest because it is small and centralized such that it is possible to think of the public service as an integrated system; other jurisdictions may struggle to centrally describe how different parts of their systems work together. Irrespective of the reason, a systematic and contingent approach to collaboration has emerged in New Zealand that illustrates the possibility of matching collaborative practices to their problem contexts.

New Zealand is a young country – first settled by humans in the thirteenth century. It was colonized by the English, and modern New Zealand was founded through a treaty between the indigenous Māori and the British Crown in 1840. For the next sixty-seven years, it was administered as a colonial outpost, before the declaration of dominion status in 1907 that formed New Zealand as a country proper. Shortly afterwards, the modern New Zealand public service was established in 1912 with the passing of the Public Service Act. This Act aimed to address the corruption, cronyism, and nepotism that had characterized the colony period and introduced a merit-based and politically neutral permanent civil service largely modelled on the Westminster and Whitehall traditions (Scott and Macaulay 2020). This foundational legislation has only been replaced three times: in 1962, when arms-length bodies were added; in 1988 when the aforementioned-NPM reforms were introduced, and in 2020 when changes were introduced to strengthen motivational and ethical foundations of the public service and create new mechanisms (based on the Toolkit) for working across agency boundaries.

2.2 The History of Interagency Collaboration in New Zealand

Throughout this history (short by the standards of most other countries), agencies have needed to work together. Two main mechanisms were traditionally employed: voluntary cooperation and structural change (see Scott and Boyd 2016 for a fuller history). Voluntary cooperation relied on the instruction from ministers, or the goodwill and social motivations of public servants, to overcome a system that was designed as a series of vertical hierarchies. In those situations where voluntary cooperation was seen as insufficient, the government would rearrange agency boundaries to place the responsibility and levers for addressing the problem within a single agency. Structural change progressively became a more and more overused lever, and between 1990 and 2010, New Zealand had more 'machinery of government' changes than any other jurisdiction (Norman and Gill 2011; Yui and Gregory 2018). However, restructuring is notoriously disruptive and expensive, and furthermore, the new boundaries would inevitably let new problems fall through the gaps (or old problems fall through new gaps). Some problems have resulted in repeated restructures with responsibility moving back and forwards between departments hoping for a perfect structure that would limit the need for working across agency boundaries – for example, the responsibility for the funding of science has moved several times while trying to achieve greater alignment with alternately the business or tertiary education sectors. Two key periods of reform were instrumental in informing a broader toolkit for interagency collaboration: Managing for Outcomes and Better Public Services.

2.2.1 Managing for Outcomes

The early 2000s saw the rise of more sustained and formalized mechanisms for working across agency boundaries, and the beginning of shared responsibilities and decision-making. New Zealand's brand of NPM was characterized by strong vertical and individual accountability for outputs (Gregory 2006). The government was concerned that this had resulted in the efficient delivery of goods and services that were not always of high value in their contribution to social outcomes (Lonti and Gregory 2007). Single-purpose agencies and single-point accountability were fracturing the public service and limiting progress on problems that crossed agency boundaries. To address these unforeseen consequences of NPM, a series of initiatives grouped under the branding 'Managing for Outcomes' attempted to improve performance by requiring agencies to describe how their outputs contributed to societal outcomes (Baehler 2003).

The cornerstone of the Managing for Outcomes reform was the introduction of Statements of Intent – a mechanism that required agencies to specify to Parliament what outcomes they were aiming to achieve and how their achievement would be measured. These new accountability mechanisms were intended to function in parallel with existing accountability mechanisms focused on service provision and expenditure. The sticking point of the new initiative was difficulty in securing commitment from chief executives to commit to outcomes that were partially dependent on the action of other agencies that they could not influence (Jensen et al. 2014). Agencies grouped themselves together to plan how they would account for 'shared outcomes', and leaders from agencies with overlapping responsibilities began to meet regularly to discuss their work. Managing for Outcomes was never formally ended but faded from government documents. Nonetheless, several of the 'Managing for Shared Outcomes' groups continued to meet – no longer to write

Statements of Intent, but instead to act as a clearing-house for resolving issues that crossed agency boundaries. These became known as 'sectors', such as the Justice Sector, the Natural Resources Sector (NRS), and the Social Sector. Sectors were not a central initiative, or even strongly encouraged from the centre, but emerged as public servants saw value in working together (Scott and Boyd 2016).

2.2.2 Better Public Services

In 2011, in the wake of the Global Financial Crisis, the New Zealand government was looking for ways to improve the affordability of public services. The Better Public Services Advisory Group met to develop options for generating more value for less money. Together, representatives from government, NGOs, and businesses determined that better collaboration would deliver the desired results. Collaboration was needed in three main areas: around a few key policy priorities that were associated with persistent social harms; around common functions, like property management, procurement, and digital technology, that were inefficient and lacked interoperability; and around joining-up frontline services to make it easier for New Zealanders to interact with government (Better Public Services Advisory Group 2011). The following period from 2012 to 2017 saw a 'let a thousand flowers bloom' approach that involved support for any-and-all efforts at improving collaboration to see what would work, as opposed to a more structured or prescriptive approach.

The Better Public Services Results programme epitomized the approach, with significant successes in measurably improving outcomes. Popular media consequently described it as the 'most significant change to how public services are delivered in New Zealand in 20 years' (Shelton 2013, p. 1). The programme involved setting ten outcome targets in areas that crossed agency and ministerial portfolio boundaries to maximize capabilities and resources. Specific ministers and chief executives were assigned to lead each result area and manage resourcing trade-offs in the environment of scarcity. Key drivers of success were reportedly the use of data and performance information; Results Action Plans that clearly outlined an intervention logic and progress measures; and a community of practice to share insights and learn from other public administrators working on interagency collaboration (Scott and Boyd 2022). Ten 'Results' were each organized using different collaborative arrangements, and therefore provided a point of contrast and opportunities for mutual learning.

Some of the corporate services like information and communications technologies (ICT), procurement, and office accommodation became the subject of a new central leadership model known as 'functional leadership', best understood as an approach to interagency collaboration involving a designated leader working to influence their peers. The approach was designed to reap the benefits of economies of scale with whole-of-government contracts that would reduce duplication, and to manage risks associated with uneven capability and practices across the public sector. Parallel roles known as 'heads of profession' developed organically around the same time, this time in areas like communications, finance, HR, legal, and policy. Each functional and professional leader employed a different operating model, with differences in their purpose, mandate, funding, and decision-making. While arrangements in this time were generally referred to as 'functional leads' and 'heads of profession', it would be a mistake to think of these as homogenous groups.

Approaches to joining-up frontline services were even more varied, with bespoke solutions popping up in various locations. Even within the same programme (e.g., 'Children's Teams' or 'Social Sector Trials'), implementation could vary significantly between one geographic region and another. The proliferation of different approaches was inefficient and often involved groups reinventing solutions, but this environment provided a fertile ground for experimentation and learning. While many attempts at collaboration withered, others blossomed.

2.3 Developing the Toolkit

New Zealand's public servants have traditionally taken an active role in driving self-reform, and the Toolkit was no exception. The reforms of the 1980s were largely proposed by the Treasury department (Scott 2001), with subsequent reforms driven by some combination of the Treasury, Department of Prime Minister and Cabinet, and the Public Service Commission (then the 'State Services Commission'). The Toolkit was developed by senior officials from the Public Service Commission (including the first author), working closely with department chief executives.

2.3.1 The Public Service Commissioner and Public Service Leadership Team

The Public Service Commissioner's role is germane to understanding the functional context of the Toolkit. While sometimes compared to the Public Service Commissioners of Australia, Canada, or Singapore, or the Civil Service Commissioner of the United Kingdom (Juillet and Rasmussen 2008), the role of the New Zealand Public Service Commissioner is significantly broader. The Public Service Commissioner is the head of the public service, with overall responsibility for (improving) its performance. The Public Service Commissioner and the State

Services Commissioner before them have long had a leadership role but were made 'head of the public service' via Cabinet directive in 2014. In 2020, a new legislation (the Public Service Act) was passed that enshrined the Commissioner as head of the public service and strengthened their responsibilities for performance and integrity.

The Commissioner is also the New Zealand government's advisor on structures and governance (elsewhere known as 'machinery of government' – Verhoest and Bouckaert 2005). These two roles mean that when either ministers or departments are faced with problems that require interagency collaboration, they seek advice from the Public Service Commission. Since 2017, this advice has been based on the Toolkit.

In 2014, the Public Service Commissioner began to convene regular gatherings of department chief executives (as the 'Public Service Leadership Team', see Scott 2019). Over time, this team took on an informal collective responsibility for supporting the Public Service Commissioner to implement public service reform (for a more detailed account of the development of the Public Service Leadership Team and the Commissioner's role with the Team, see Scott and Macaulay 2020).

In 2017, at one such strategic retreat, this leadership team turned their attention to the matter of collaboration across the public service. Through discussion they concluded that they and their agencies were good at collaborating when the collaboration did not require significant trade-offs against their core agency work and could be done with voluntary, informal, or 'soft' coordination. They also had experience and competence in reorganizing or restructuring to form new agencies to focus on specific issues (the 'hard' approach), but they recognized the disruption and costs involved in this, as well as the risk of unforeseen consequences of new boundaries. They therefore understood the importance of using 'hard' approaches sparingly in practice. This left a gap of expertise for working in the 'middle' ground of collaboration, where they still felt substantial challenges for collaborating in semi-structured ways. (Note this account relies on an interview with a public servant present at the retreat.)

2.3.2 Searching for the Middle

However, chief executives' collective experiences indicated that there were examples of successful 'middle' ground collaborations scattered across the public service. Members of the team had each personally contributed to collaborative successes over their careers spanning forty years, but they acknowledged that the insights from some of those successful collaborations were not well captured or disseminated across the public service. Having assumed responsibility through their charter for improving the collaborative capacity of the public service through their agencies, the Public Sector Leadership Team saw their task as bringing those initiatives together to learn from them. This broadened into a process that included a team of experienced public servants who could help them identify some of these examples of successful interagency collaboration.

The project team was led by Rodney Scott (the first author of this Element) and included other senior public servants Callum Butler, Ross Boyd, Hugh Oliver, and Hugo Vitalis. Margaret Mabbett and Maddy Lee were subsequently involved in drafting guidance documents that allowed public servants to use the Toolkit more easily in designing their own interagency collaborative arrangements. The team included three people who had each been responsible for key interagency collaboration programmes in the past. Ross Boyd led the Better Public Services Results programme; Hugh Oliver proposed much of the functional leadership and head of profession models; and Hugo Vitalis led advice on local and place-based models to join-up services at the front line. Together with the chief executives in the Public Service Leadership Team, the project team were familiar with decades of successes and failures in cross-agency work.

What the Public Service Leadership Team originally imagined was a simple collation of case studies that demonstrated the different ways in which successful collaboration had been sustained, or that captured the lessons from adaptive management of collaborative practice that became more successful over time. Workshops in June and July 2017 identified dozens of examples of interagency collaboration in the New Zealand public service dating back to 2004. As the examples were described, it became apparent that solutions clustered into different broad types. About a third of the examples involved a few agencies collaborating to plan and oversee the achievement of a public policy objective. Similarly, approximately a third involved most or all central government agencies working together on common functions, processes, or professional disciplines. The remaining third were mostly examples of agencies working together to deliver more aligned or joined-up services, collaborating around the needs of individuals. In each instance, the lessons that were drawn from the successful examples were more similar within those three groups than between them. These subsequently became the three categories in the vertical axis of the Toolkit.

2.3.3 The Emergence of Contingency

This simple observation, that solutions clustered together by problem type, was the impetus for a contingent approach. The creation of these three categories was inductive and somewhat accidental. However, after discussing this observation, the team's aim was no longer simply to assemble a collection of examples that may serve as inspiration for future endeavours, but instead to provide something more instructional: 'for these types of problem contexts, these solutions tend to be more successful'. Public Service Commission Policy Manager (and project team member) Hugo Vitalis noted that the aims of the project were lifted: 'We started to wonder whether we could create some sort of heuristic that, even if it was a bit fuzzy in parts, provided some sense of guidance or direction.'

Having discovered three categories of solution by accident, the hunt was on for further ways in which problem contexts could be matched to solutions. Various existing frameworks were considered, like Wilson's production/procedure framework (1989), Kurtz and Snowden's 'Cynefin' framework for sensemaking (2003), and Donahue's (2004) framework for collaborative governance, but none were a good fit for the examples. The Public Service Leadership Team had repeatedly come back to the idea of 'soft', 'middle', and 'hard', describing the governance or decision-making mechanisms relating to the collaboration, but these were categories of solution, not of the problem context. Eventually, the team observed that 'harder' solutions were required when collaboration required agencies to sacrifice or trade-off their individual agency priorities and autonomy in service to the shared collaborative goals. Ross Boyd, Programme Manager of the Better Public Service Results Programme, observed that 'the more that agencies needed to sacrifice, the more formal the powers and accountabilities needed to be'. This idea of trade-off or sacrifice was explored and found to be a good match for differentiating the various experiences of collaboration. The examples could then be grouped into a two-dimensional framework: the type of problem on the vertical axis, and the required degree of trade-off (and therefore formal accountability) on the horizontal axis (see Figure 2).

'Softer' solutions were cheaper and easier but were only effective when trade-offs with core agency work were not too significant. As the degree of trade-off rose, the softer collaborative methods tended to break down. Among the higher levels of trade-off required, more formal ('harder') mechanisms were necessary for allowing ministers and other decision-makers to reconcile their individual agency priorities and develop accountability mechanisms for achieving their shared agency priorities.

In each category, the corresponding examples were distilled into a few key elements. In some instances, there were no ideal or wholly successful cases, and so the most successful elements of several examples were combined. Sometimes this could be informed by formal evaluations, but in other instances, the team relied on expert judgement from experienced practitioners. On each

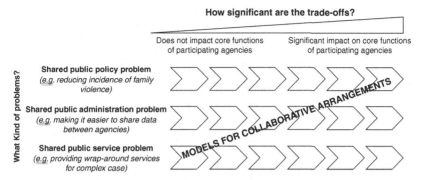

Figure 2 Framework for contingent collaboration

horizontal line, six different collaborative models were identified, ranging from 'soft', informal or voluntary models to 'hard', structural reorganization. The two extremes of the spectrum represent traditional approaches to the organization and operation of individual agencies (voluntary coordination and restructuring), and the four intermediate or 'middle' solutions were more recent additions to the suite of options available to public servants in configuring interagency collaboration (see Table 1).

Although the horizontal axis of the Toolkit is presented as a linear spectrum from soft to hard, it can also be imagined as a loop or horseshoe. That is, whenever the government resorts to hard structural change, this creates new boundaries between separate agencies, often with a new set of problems that span those boundaries. Nonetheless, the arrangement of the Toolkit as a grid was thought to be the simplest and clearest way to convey information to public managers.

Under the leadership of Public Service Commissioner Peter Hughes, the Toolkit and descriptions of the embedded elements were tested extensively with the Public Service Leadership Team and individuals involved in the leadership of each example referenced. Between July and September, the team engaged broadly with experienced practitioners across the public service, including a sub-group of chief executives, before launching the Toolkit at a Public Service Leadership Team retreat in October 2017, and publishing it on the Public Service Commission website in January 2018.

2.4 Using the Toolkit

The Chief Executives saw the Toolkit as addressing two key challenges: helping agencies to understand when to use which collaborative models, and to elevate the profile of middle solutions as the result of an intentional design choice. Where middle solutions had been used previously, they were grouped with

Table 1 EEighteen models for organizing government

	Soft		Middle		Hard	
Policy problems	Agencies planning separately	Voluntary coordination	Shared responsibility	Collective accountability	Semi-structural integration	Structural integration
Administration problems	Agencies functioning separately	Voluntary club	Functional lead/head of profession	System leader	Internal regulator/monitor	Shared functions
Delivery problems	Agencies delivering separately	Co-location	Collective impact network	Collective impact board	Federated services	Delivery vehicles

purely voluntary 'soft' solutions and seen as a lower priority than individual agency work. Chief executives saw the act of creating a toolkit as a way to give middle solutions legitimacy as part of the formal machinery of government.

Rather than launch the Toolkit with a publicized roll-out, the Public Service Commission waited for agencies to identify problems that required collaborative solutions, and then introduced them to the Toolkit to help them navigate through their problem. The Toolkit then gradually permeated agency discussions around collaborative arrangements. At the time of writing, it continues to be the basis of advice to government on how to solve problems that span agency boundaries. The Minister of Public Services, Chris Hipkins (2019a, p. 4), described the importance of the Toolkit: 'The agility and adaptability of the public service can be improved both by providing alternative options to the creation of new departments and introducing flexible mechanisms to support more effective and sustainable joint working.'

2.4.1 Down and Across

For public service practitioners, the Toolkit is intended to operate as a heuristic to help them confront an unstructured problem and order it through a series of questions into a framing structure that will maximize opportunities to address it. Practitioners needed to decide, based on their problem context, how far 'down' and then how far 'across' the Toolkit would provide the most promising solution.

Guidance instructed practitioners to first consider what kind of problem they were trying to solve and use this to identify which horizontal line of the Toolkit was most relevant. Were they working with a few agencies at a national level to solve a policy problem; working with many agencies on common functions or capabilities to solve an administrative problem; or working at the front line to solve a service coordination problem?

Having chosen which horizontal line was most relevant to the problem they were trying to solve, practitioners were then given prompts to identify which Toolkit column was most relevant, from 'soft' voluntary models through a spectrum to 'hard' structural models. Increasingly 'harder' models were required when participating agencies needed to make difficult choices between their individual agency goals and collaborative goals. Harder models are more expensive, take up more managerial attention, and require the investment of political capital. Therefore, practitioners should choose the softest model that is likely to be sufficient given the degree of trade-off required, and for which there is sufficient political priority. This exposes a core tension – there will be some problems that cannot be solved with soft models, but where there is not sufficient political will for hard models. In these situations, practitioners may need to consider alternate goals or else wait for the opportunities to ripen.

The models described in the Toolkit are 'ideal types' rather than being prescriptive or rule-based. It is designed as a flexible tool, which may be applied differently throughout the life cycle of a collaborative initiative depending on which model is most appropriate – for example, the easiest improvements may be achieved using 'softer' models, but later improvements may involve agency sacrifices and require 'harder' governance models to achieve. For example, the Justice Sector, described in Section 3, began in 2003 as 'Voluntary Coordination' model before formalizing in 2012 as a 'Shared Responsibility' model around shared targets for crime reduction. Similarly, the social sector had operated as a 'Shared Responsibility' model but was unable to jointly agree to the selection of priority population groups; they later formed into the Social Wellbeing Board (an example of the 'Collective Accountability' model), where the board reported collectively to a superordinate minister.

Some problems are best conceived of (and addressed) as a collection of related or nested elements; for example, a 'hard' model may be required to achieve a carbon-neutral public service, within the context of a broader (soft) voluntary collaboration around issues relating to environmental management. Additionally, some problems operate at multiple levels, for example, requiring policy agreement at a national level as well as collective action at a frontline level. For example, social sector priorities agreed by the Social Wellbeing Board on the top layer of the Toolkit were addressed through frontline service collaboration (the South Auckland Wellbeing Board) described in the bottom layer.

Even while using the Toolkit, selecting the right collaborative model still requires management 'craft' (Bardach 1998). However, the Toolkit has been welcomed by practitioners as at least providing a starting guide. One public servant described the Toolkit as providing 'a framework to step through different structural and governance elements in a way that makes sense and helps people develop options and advice that really addresses the context they are working in'. When considering the usefulness of the Toolkit, the relevant comparison is not perfection, but instead the absence of a contingent framework at all. Another public servant commented that 'agencies really appreciate having a structure or framework to help them work out what to do'.

2.4.2 Ongoing Refinement

The Toolkit was based on past experiences and then used to inform the design of future collaborative arrangements (or the modification of existing arrangements).

Past examples included things that worked well, and other things that did not, so from the beginning the Toolkit involved a mix of proven, mature models, and less mature models that were still being refined.

Since its launch in 2017, the Toolkit has been used to design dozens of collaborative arrangements. In some cases, the proposed models did not quite work as intended. Some models required messy workarounds to engineer joint decision-making and responsibility – solutions that worked against the prevailing policies.

In 2020, the New Zealand Parliament passed a new Public Service Act and amended the Public Finance Act. This enabled changes to three models in the Toolkit: Executive Boards, System Leads, and Interagency Ventures. When proposing these legislative changes to Cabinet, Minister of State Services Chris Hipkins described the Toolkit in detail and praised it as having 'helped [the government] to more effectively apply the range of models' (Hipkins 2019a, p. 4). However, he argued that legislative changes would help with 'commitment problems, a lack of stability over time, and prioritization of departmental responsibilities over joint working' (p. 5).

In contrast, some see the reliance on formal structures as a weakness, reflecting a continuation of the NPM preoccupation with accountability. Eppel and O'Leary ask, 'has New Zealand legislated collaboration to death? Will so many centralized rules and regulations have to be followed to allow collaboration that the creativity that comes from bottom-up collaboration will be stunted?' (2021, p. 66).

3 Interagency Collaboration for Public Policy

> Collaboration is never easy ... so why do some people remain committed to the goal?
>
> *(Ross Boyd, programme manager of the Better Public Services Results Programme)*

This section deals with models for addressing shared public policy problems (see Table 2). The New Zealand public service has approximately thirty-five departments, with related and overlapping policy responsibilities. For example, the Ministry for the Environment, Department of Conservation, and Ministry for Primary Industries all have responsibility for environmental resources. The Ministry of Justice, Police, and Department of Corrections all have responsibilities relating to criminal justice. Interagency collaboration around a policy problem typically involves a few agencies working together.

Cross-sector work competes for attention, resource, and decisions, with those policy priorities assigned by ministers to individual agencies. New Zealand Police Chief Andrew Coster reflected: 'The biggest challenge I think in working

Table 2 Models for organizing around public policy problems

Non-collaborative	Softer			Harder
Agencies planning separately	Voluntary coordination	Shared responsibility	Collective accountability	Semi-structural integration	Structural integration

cross sector is reconciling the individual agencies' accountabilities in part of a bigger work programme or focus. The reality of our system is that ministers have priorities they want to deliver with their agencies and a sector approach calls for us to work our sector priorities in against those individual agency goals.'

The collaborative models in this layer of the toolkit all involve some variation of shared responsibility. The aim is to make representatives of separate agencies feel invested in solving a problem together (Scott and Boyd 2020). Individual responsibility is much clearer, and there are greater coordination and commitment problems the more parties are involved. As group size increases, coordination costs tend to rise (Van Huyck et al. 1990; Weber et al. 2021) and felt responsibility tends to fall (Ingham et al. 1974). The 'softer', less formal models rely on reciprocal altruism (Oliver 2019) and goodwill. Middle solutions assign shared or joint responsibility for specific outcomes. Harder solutions group organizations together under a superordinate structure.

Each of the models described in this section relies on consensus – progress is limited by the extent to which the different agencies can reach an agreement. The extent of that consensus is determined by the degree of overlap, and some models for collaboration require consensus on only a few items while allowing divergence in areas where there is less interdependence (Susskind et al. 1999; Emerson et al. 2012). However, across all models, collaboration is an ongoing process of negotiation (Thomson and Perry 2006) with associated transaction and coordination costs (Van Huyck et al. 1990; Ren et al. 2005). One of the key costs is time, corresponding to the seniority of those involved. For the most senior decision-makers, this time not only has a financial cost but detracts from a finite well of attention for other issues that government must manage. Other costs are emotional – the frustration and distrust that come from uncertainty of the goodwill or reliability of collaboration partners (Doberstein 2016; Scott and Bardach 2019). These models encourage public managers to think carefully about where collaboration is needed and to specify the areas of shared responsibility as narrowly as possible. The leadership competencies involved in successfully implementing these models are based around a comfort with sharing power.

As with each layer, the public policy layer consists nominally of six models. We say 'nominally', because the first and sixth models are not collaborative at all. The first model, 'agencies planning separately', describes the status quo of individual agency responses to policy problems. The remaining models involve increasing formalized ways of deciding policy responses to cross-cutting problems. The sixth model, 'structural integration', involves redrawing agency boundaries such that the problem in question no longer crosses agency boundaries. Talbot and Talbot (2013) explore mergers between departments as a possible

Table 3 Agencies planning separately model

Collaboration context	History of successful single-agency working
Problem type	Problems and policy areas fall within the responsibility of a single agency
Planning and activity	As normal
Agreement on goals and outcomes	Budget processes, appropriations, ministerial priorities
Governance	Agency hierarchies
Ministerial relationships	Separately to separate ministers
Incentives	Annual reporting and audit, ministerial accountability, recognition of chief executives
Funding	Through individual agency appropriation

solution to boundary-crossing problems, although inevitably this means that other problems will cross boundaries of the new structure, and governments need to be able to traverse these boundaries without constant reorganization.

The following sections provide a brief description of each of the models in the public policy layer of the Toolkit. Tables 3–8 (and equivalent tables in Sections 4 and 5) are drawn directly from the Toolkit (State Services Commission 2018) and describe each model's characteristics in terms of its collaboration context, problem type, methods of planning, agreement on goals and outcomes, governance arrangements, ministerial relationships, management incentives, and funding options. In each of the collaborative models, this is accompanied by an illustrative example. Note that claims of effectiveness and applicability in Sections 3–5 refer to the judgements of the project team that developed the Toolkit, and not to scholarly claims.

3.1 Agencies Planning Separately

Planning separately constitutes the traditional approach to managing public policy problems (Table 3). It is effective in cases when problems fall clearly within the remit of an existing agency, without interdependencies into other agencies and without significant trade-off against the single agency's other priorities. Its processes and functions will be familiar to practitioners and academics alike, being reproduced across the public service and largely based on traditional organizational theory. Agreement on goals and outcomes is secured through conventional budget processes and ministerial priorities. Governance is conducted through typical agency hierarchies, and relationships with political principals run separately to separate ministers. Incentives are

Table 4 Voluntary coordination model

Collaboration context	Natural grouping of agencies involved in the problem, with strong working relationships
Problem type	Does not require significant trade-offs between agency and collective interests, manageable mostly within baselines
Planning and activity	Coordination of work with common interests and resources
Agreement on goals and outcomes	Opportunistic, within areas of overlapping interest
Governance	Cross-agency cooperation/coordination, without collective decision-making authority
Ministerial relationships	Separately with each minister of a relevant portfolio
Incentives	Absence of trade-offs, individual or lead agency accountability
Funding	Agency baselines

provided by accountability processes like annual reporting and audit, and individual ministerial responsibility, as well as recognition (primarily for chief executives). Funding takes the form of individual agency appropriations.

3.2 Voluntary Coordination

Voluntary coordination involves agencies working together in a loose and unstructured way without formal mandate or obligation (Table 4). This model is primarily used where various agencies have a common interest around which their respective work can be aligned. The aim is to support each agency's separate goals more efficiently, absent significant trade-offs between individual and collective agency interests. It is important that each agency's contribution is manageable within their existing baseline funding and priorities. There is no collective decision-making authority, which may in turn limit resource sharing. Groups of agencies engaging in Voluntary Coordination are likely to be focused on improving alignment and addressing tensions between conflicting functions within participating agencies. Progress depends on constructive relationships and trust between partners.

Voluntary Coordination may benefit from the presence of a 'lead agency' seen as having the most 'skin in the game' (interview, Callum Butler), in order to simplify administration and maintain progress. Giving a lead agency responsibility for coordinating activity introduces a corresponding responsibility on the chief executive (CE) and minister of that agency to provide quality advice in relation to that shared activity. The alternative is for agencies to remain separately accountable to individual ministers. The simpler lines of accountability provide little incentive for cross-agency work but also minimize the administrative barriers to getting started.

This model can be adapted for use either in short-term policy development or on a longer-term/ongoing basis to address shared problems as they arise. The model is appropriate for the involvement of many agencies, as the benefits of accessing additional resources tend to outweigh the additional administrative costs. While the 'shared responsibility' and 'collective accountability' models have only been effective with two to five members, 'voluntary voordination' has been effective with up to ten contributing agencies. Limitations of this model largely arise from the informality and voluntary nature of the arrangements: agency work tends to trump interagency work, and progress relies on continued attention by key individuals.

· 3.2.1 Case Study: The Natural Resources Sector

The NRS is the group of agencies with overlapping responsibility for New Zealand's natural resources. Conversations between senior public servants at the Department of Conservation, Ministry for the Environment, and Ministry for Primary Industries revealed overlaps and tensions within the sector's work. James Palmer, who was Deputy Secretary for Sector Strategy at the Ministry for the Environment at the time, observed that agencies were increasingly 'bumping up against each other'. Ministers too were fed up with conflicting advice from different agencies, and applied pressure on chief executives to produce something more coherent.

Since 2008, there have been regular meetings of chief executives and deputies from seven agencies: Department of Conservation; Department of Internal Affairs; Land Information New Zealand; Ministry of Business, Innovation and Employment; Ministry for the Environment; Ministry for Primary Industries; and Te Puni Kōkiri (Ministry of Māori Affairs).

A Support Unit oversees the work programme of the Sector, providing a strategic view of priority issues. The unit is jointly funded but housed by the Ministry for the Environment. Part of the unit's role is to champion collaborative approaches and build commonality within the NRS, which was considered important due to the added difficulty of collaboration with limited resourcing.

One of the key successes of the NRS was participation in joint budget processes across the sector. According to James, this involved successfully consolidating different needs, 'forcing everyone to prioritise and plan together' and resulted in shared advice to ministers on funding priorities. Some of the impetus for this came from the ministers involved, whose sponsorship was 'hugely important . . . it takes discipline on behalf of ministers to be committed to the success of other departments as much as for their own'. Perhaps even more significantly, 'policy got more collaborative in (key priorities) like freshwater and climate change, and that stood the test of time'.

One of the key insights drawn from the experience of the NRS is that collaborative operations will need to have different expectations for different types of work, even within the same model. James observed, 'times when you need lots of oversight and sponsorship, times when it can be very loose and cooperative, times when you can make joint decisions, and times when you want one person to make decisions'.

3.3 Shared Responsibility

When agencies cannot reconcile their different needs to achieve a common goal through voluntary coordination, they may need to take shared responsibility (Table 5). This model is appropriate for balancing shared planning and resourcing with aligned but separate delivery. It is generally most effective when the shared outcome can be achieved by a few key agencies working together with shared responsibility.

The model does not require Cabinet or legislative mandate, and most commonly arises from self-organization, where chief executives form a board to agree on collective goals and measures to track performance on problems that they all hold some lever for addressing. Such a board will often be supported by multiple levels of collaborative governance arrangements – most likely working groups and a jointly resourced secretariat, and in some cases an informal group of ministers that reflects the remit of the CE board. The diagram in Figure 3 provides an illustration of the possible governance levels.

This model can effectively use more formal arrangements than purely voluntary measures, as long as the relevant issues can be more tightly defined and involve only a few essential agencies. Mechanisms like setting targets, agreeing performance measures, and providing joint advice serve to build commitment and focus among participating agencies. This model is most effective when that focus and commitment are distributed evenly among the agencies.

The shared responsibility required among chief executives in this model may result in complexities due to the mingling of horizontal accountabilities with more traditional vertical ones. Chief executives are forced to rely on each other, without having the power to influence each other's actions as they

Table 5 Shared responsibility model

Collaboration context	Voluntary solutions have been inadequate, CEs are willing to take shared responsibility
Problem type	A specific cross-cutting persistent policy problem that is important enough to warrant bringing CEs together
Planning and activity	CE group from relevant agencies coordinate their decision rights towards the agreed problem definition
Agreement on goals and outcomes	Common definitions and descriptions of target groups and results, being selective about priorities, collectively agree to measures and confirm with ministers
Governance	Collaborative governance through a group of critical CEs for setting strategy and signalling agency commitment can have a chair within that group, working groups at other levels with clear delegated decision rights, jointly resourced co-located secretariat and/or policy advisory function
Ministerial relationships	Shared advice to ministers on areas of joint responsibility, corresponding (informal) ministerial group for managing trade-offs
Incentives	Collective responsibility for priority results, reporting to ministers, and recognition for CEs
Funding	Any of the following: joint resourcing/staffing for shared activities, specific activities funded from agency baselines, agreed contributions, or pooled underspends

would for people within their own agency. Informal groups of ministers can be useful in resolving tensions between different accountabilities within and across agencies.

3.3.1 Case Study: Justice Sector Board

While some 'shared responsibility' groups were configured around temporary priorities in a time-limited way, others have proven remarkably stable over time. The Justice Sector has existed in some form or another from 2003 until the time of writing. The Justice Sector Leadership Board is a group of chief executives (New Zealand Police, Ministry of Justice, Department of Corrections, Serious Fraud Office, Crown Law Office) that coordinate reforms intended to 'improve

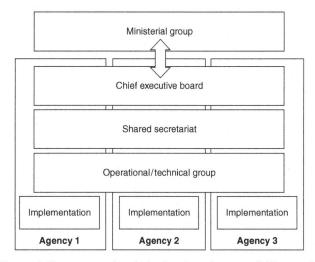

Figure 3 Governance levels in the shared responsibility model

services, reduce harm and the number of people in the criminal justice system, maintain institutions and manage investment' (Ministry of Justice 2021). Over this period, the individual leaders have all changed multiple times, yet the group remains. Former Justice Sector Group Manager Paul O'Connell attributes this stability to solid governance processes: 'The more you can solidify processes that outlive given personalities, then so long as everybody doesn't change at once, you've got a chance that the process and "the way things are done around here" endures beyond a given individual.'

Members of the Justice Sector recognized that police, courts, and corrections officers all rely very heavily on hierarchy to get things done and had a predisposition to adhere to processes that translated into how they collaborated with each other. The Board operated under a comprehensive Terms of Reference that set out its purpose, membership, accountabilities (collectively, of the chair, and of individual members), support arrangements, meeting schedule, and communication principles. As Aphra Green, General Manager of Sector Strategy, put it: 'Sticking quite rigidly to the format of papers, who needs to be consulted on papers, timeliness of papers for those groups, has been really important to the functioning of the sector and to everyone feeling like there's a high level of trust and confidence.'

Others attribute its persistence to the galvanizing effect of a clear mission and shared metaphor. The Board was based on a collective conception of justice system operating as a 'pipeline' through which individuals progress. This clear articulation of linear interdependence was effective at securing members' commitment to the cross-agency work. Deputy Secretary of Police, Audrey Sonerson, reflected on the need to 'work out what are the things that will pull it together, what are the things that will keep it together, and what are the things that will transcend the personal relationships over time?'

The Justice Sector Board forms part of a cascading governance arrangement. Chief executives meet every two months and collectively brief their respective ministers after each meeting. This collective brief is a departure from standard New Zealand practice, where chief executives each brief their respective ministers separately. At the next level, deputy chief executives meet every two weeks to drive the work programme set by the chief executives, while a wider group of stakeholders meet every two months. Support for the governance mechanism is provided by an operational team known as the Justice Sector Group, made up of officials from across the Justice Sector and hosted by the Ministry of Justice. Its functions include policy and data analysis and measurement that form the basis of strategic and investment advice. Oliver Valins, Deputy Chief Executive of Crown Law noted that 'you don't get [that many] . . . agencies of that size working together without an awful lot of things that happen in the background . . . none of that stuff happens just because a chief executive sits in a room and wishes it so'.

The Board was funded through a joint funding arrangement set up in April 2012. The fund allowed unspent money from the Justice Sector to be saved and invested in future initiatives, which would otherwise have been returned to the Treasury. Being able to share savings gave the Justice Sector the flexibility to invest in interventions that delivered better results, redistributing money saved by one agency to fund another's initiatives working towards the same overall goal of reducing crime. Police Chief Andrew Coster emphasized that the fund 'provided the opportunity to do some novel things . . . a little bit outside of our normal areas of accountability'. He contrasted this experience to the usual difficulty that agencies face in reprioritizing budgets towards innovative approaches.

3.4 Collective Accountability

The collective accountability model involves a statutory board made up of chief executives from various agencies (Table 6). It is used to assign collective accountability to that group of chief executives for a specific purpose, providing a formal mechanism for cross-agency decision-making. This is particularly useful for addressing complex issues with impacts and policy levers that sit across agencies and ministerial portfolios. As with the shared responsibility model, it might be used to strengthen cross-agency planning and resourcing for a common goal, but where the trade-offs are so difficult that only a formal and

Table 6 Collective accountability model

Collaboration context	Complex relationships and deep trade-offs between individual and collective interests. Shared responsibility has been insufficient
Problem type	Large and important problem that warrants additional priority, cost, and time; unsolvable through reframing to involve fewer agencies
Planning and activity	Priorities and terms of reference agreed by Cabinet for a board of CEs
Agreement on goals and outcomes	Cabinet decisions on performance results and targets; cabinet agreement on purpose, scope and functions on establishment; ministerial priorities; budget process
Governance	Cabinet-established board and set mandates and responsibilities, may include shifting decision rights. CEs responsible to the minister for the functions of the board
Ministerial relationships	Directly to one lead minister who has overall responsibility for the board and priority results
Incentives	Ministerial accountability, recognition for CEs, potential for scheduled reporting to Cabinet, Cabinet-agreed investment plans, annual reporting and audit, public reporting on progress, and influence of results and reputation on availability of future resources
Funding	Either the board administers its own appropriation or uses shared responsibility model options for appropriations from another agency

legal accountability is sufficient to ensure that collective work takes precedence over individual agency work. The collective accountability board formalizes decision-making for strategy, planning, and resourcing. Responsibility for the delivery of services related to the board's priorities remains with individual agencies (see Figure 4).

Collective accountability boards are established by Cabinet decision followed by an Order in Council (a legislative instrument). The responsibilities of the board to its minister are set out in legislation, and its scope and functions are agreed upon by Cabinet at the time of establishment. The chief executives within the board's remit must implement the board's decisions, including consulting with the chief executives of any other affected agencies.

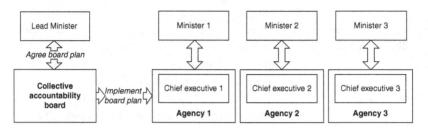

Figure 4 Collective accountability board governance structure

3.4.1 Border Executive Board

Between 2012 and 2020, various parts of the New Zealand government had used elements of the collective accountability model (notably the Social Wellbeing Board), but never to the full extent described in the 2020 revision of the Toolkit. The first example of a statutory board under the Public Service Act 2020 was the Border Executive Board.

Several agencies have overlapping responsibilities regarding the passage of goods and people across the national border. The Border Sector Governance Group, broadly an example of the 'Voluntary Coordination' model, had been in place since 2007. However, this group had suffered from reliance on a lead agency, with variable levels of input and support from other participating agencies. The Border Executive Board was established by Cabinet in January 2021, with joint accountability for strategic border improvements as managed by a Border Sector Strategy against which performance is monitored and supplemented by user experience data. The Board advises on investment decisions relating to the border system, identifying and managing any gaps in the integration of health and risk management, particularly in the context of the COVID-19 pandemic.

Members of the board are the chief executives of Ministry of Business, Innovation and Employment; Ministry of Foreign Affairs and Trade; Ministry of Health; Ministry for Primary Industries; Ministry of Transport; and the New Zealand Customs Service, with this chief executive acting as the chair. Together, the board administers its own separate budget appropriation, to be used for providing advice on policy and investment and contributing to the design and coordination of joint border initiatives. As the board matures, it is intended that the appropriation will expire and the board will shift to being club-funded from the participating agencies' baselines.

The board is supported by a group of senior officials and a secretariat. The senior officials' group facilitates the implementation of the board's work programme, developing an initial programme to put to the board, providing updates, addressing emerging barriers, and overseeing assurance and audit work.

Table 7 Semi-structural integration model

Collaboration context	Previous experience suggests a CE and minister are needed without new department or arms-length body
Problem type	Either stable, cohesive policy settings or activity is definable, measurable and severable from functions of a host department
Planning and activity	Consolidation and demarcation of functions from other agencies
Agreement on goals and outcomes	Budget process of appropriations and ministerial priorities
Governance	Quasi-departmental structure supported by a host agency. Either led by its own CE or a director who reports to the CE of host agency
Ministerial relationships	Direct line of accountability to a responsible minister
Incentives	Annual reporting and audit, ministerial accountability, recognition for CEs
Funding	Individual agency appropriation administered by host department

The secretariat provides administrative support for board meetings as well as facilitating matters between agencies, monitoring and reporting on progress and risk, and supporting the minister responsible for the board with papers as required. As the Border Executive Board is a relatively new structure at the time of writing, participants were not able to offer reflections on what has worked or not so far, nor why.

3.5 Semi-structural Integration

Sometimes two agencies can work more closely together by placing one inside the other. A small specialist agency that needs to work closely with a larger agency can be nested within it (Table 7). By working within the platform and operating environment of the host agency, the nested agency engages in more tacit knowledge sharing. This is not a model suited to all cases but provides an alternative to full structural integration that allows the nested agency to retain its identity, profile, and focus. The Toolkit refers to this as 'semi-structural integration', although perhaps 'structural semi-integration' would have been more appropriate, as the nested agency retains some features of a separate agency and some features of integration within the host.

The nested agency remains operationally autonomous but is legally considered part of that host agency. The leader of the nested agency is still titled chief executive, has a direct line of ministerial accountability, and has control over relevant resources. The minister accountable for the departmental agency may be different from the minister responsible for the host department. Nonetheless, the nested agency typically operates within the strategic intentions, corporate platform, and planning and reporting context of the host agency (see Figure 5).

The model allows for slight variations in the level of autonomy of the nested department. In some cases, the host agency will hold ultimate responsibility for funding; in others, the nested agency can be set up with the capability to manage its own funding, including assets and liabilities, answering directly to the responsible minister for what it achieves with this funding. In some cases, the host will set the overall strategic intentions for itself and the nested agency and report these to Parliament; in other cases, these are done separately.

This model comes with similar limitations to those of the structural integration approach. Bringing two agencies together does not do anything to help either agency engage further with other agencies outside that semi-structural integration. Any configuration of agency boundaries inevitably divides policy problems imperfectly.

At the time of writing, there were five examples of Semi-structural Integration. The Cancer Control Agency is nested within the Ministry of Health, providing

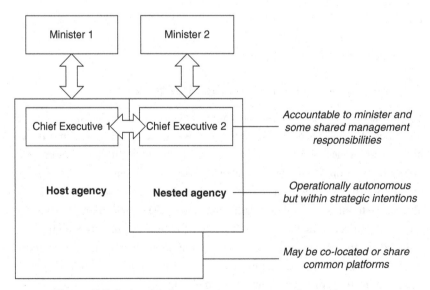

Figure 5 Relationship between host agency and nested agency

a dedicated focus on cancer but remaining linked to other parts of the health system. The Ministry of Ethnic Communities is nested in the Department of Internal Affairs, which has responsibility for the NGO and community sectors. The National Emergency Management Agency is nested within the Department of Prime Minister and Cabinet so it can coordinate a whole-of-government response to emergencies. The Office for Māori Crown Relations ('Te Arawhiti') is nested within the Ministry of Justice and provides linkages between the Waitangi Tribunal, the Justice Sector, and the public service more broadly. Finally, the Social Wellbeing Agency is nested within the Public Service Commission.

3.5.1 Case Study: Social Wellbeing Agency

Of the five extant examples of semi-structural integration, the Social Wellbeing Agency is the oldest, established in 2017. The agency was intended to work alongside other, larger agencies and non-governmental organizations to improve data and evidence-based decision-making and better join-up the social sector. The agency is hosted by the Public Service Commission, intended to indicate independence and a neutral view of the sector, instead of being aligned to any individual social sector agency. In some ways, this hosting arrangement makes the Social Wellbeing Agency an imperfect example of semi-structural integration for the purpose of collaborating because its host agency is not its closest collaborator. Despite this, the Social Wellbeing Agency is the most mature example, and other examples are still evolving.

The Social Wellbeing Agency (originally named the Social Investment Agency) leads the government's social wellbeing approach, delivering data-driven insights to decision-makers. Ultimately, the Agency's level of separation from other social sector agencies is a mixed blessing; it provided the Agency with the desired independence from the social sector but at the expense of integration. The founding Chief Executive, Dorothy Adams, observed:

> We could try new things in our early days that it was more difficult for a large agency like the Ministry of Social Development to do because we could be agile and take more risks. But what I learned from that is that you can't go too far ahead of the bigger agencies or else it's very hard to bring them on board afterwards. When we wanted to take experiments to scale, the other agencies just found that the jump could be too big. In hindsight we should have got them involved earlier, because without the bigger agencies we couldn't take anything to scale.

At the time of writing, the Social Wellbeing Agency was considering how it could reconfigure to be more closely connected to the other social sector agencies.

3.6 Structural Integration

Structural integration constitutes a full circle back to a reliance on individual agencies that incorporate responsibilities for all or most parts of an identified public policy issue (Table 8). It is best used in cases where all other solutions, including organizational arrangements from throughout this section, have been tried without sufficient success. Regardless of how it's achieved, the creation of a new agency inevitably involves significant cost, disruption, and reorganization. It therefore requires the identified issue to be the most important way to organize resources, over and above these other considerations. Once established, the usual processes for a single agency apply to agreement on goals and outcomes, governance, incentives, and funding.

Table 8 Structural integration model

Collaboration context	All other solutions have been tried
Problem type	Problem is the most important way to organize agencies; justifies significant cost, disruption and reorganization; functions and activities can be clearly defined and integrated
Planning and activity	Merger, takeover, or new agency to consolidate activity relating to the problem
Agreement on goals and outcomes	Budget process of appropriations and ministerial priorities
Governance	Direct line of accountability to a minister responsible for the agency and portfolio ministers for specific functions
Ministerial relationship	Minister responsible for the agency, possibly portfolio ministers for separate functions
Incentives	Annual reporting and audit, ministerial accountability, CE recognition
Funding	Individual appropriation for the new agency

4 Interagency Collaboration for Public Administration

Aligning systems and processes involves compromises, and a willingness to let go of absolute control.

(Hugh Oliver, lead advisor on the functional leadership model)

The second layer of the Toolkit deals with models for addressing shared public administration problems, typically relating to common functions (like property

Table 9 Models for organizing around public administration problems

Non-collaborative	Softer				Harder
Agencies functioning separately	Voluntary club	Functional lead/ head of profession	System leader	Internal regulator/ monitor	Shared functions

management, procurement, or information and communication technology) or common professions (like legal advice, human resource management, or finance, see Table 9). It is often inefficient to have thirty-five different approaches to, for example, government procurement across the thirty-five agencies, and there may not be the critical mass in each agency to ensure the capability to manage procurement effectively. Therefore, New Zealand (like many other jurisdictions) has been experimenting with more coordinated or collective approaches to the delivery of or capability within common functions and professional services. As with the first layer, models in the Toolkit constitute a spectrum from soft to hard, between agencies operating entirely separately, and a fully shared services model where one agency delivers the function on behalf of all others.

New Zealand, as a rule, does not favour generic one-size solutions, as this constrains the ability of the leaders of individual agencies to run their operations flexibly and effectively, preferring more informal or voluntary solutions than would be chosen in comparable jurisdictions (e.g., the UK Civil Service Functional and Professional Model, see Thornton 2018). Despite not generally favouring one solution, public servants recognize that thirty-five different solutions are rarely necessary. As Government Chief Accountant Paul Helm observed 'I don't favour one solution for everyone – of course you can have a spread. But in most situations, I don't think you need too much of a spread; I always ask people why they are specialising if we've got 90% commonality.'

As compared to the public policy layer of the Toolkit, models in the public policy layer often involve more agencies. For example, while five agencies may have a shared interest in freshwater management, all thirty-five agencies have computers and would benefit from improved information and communication technology capability. This leads to another key distinction between layers: policy problems involving a few agencies can be managed by shared responsibility and consensus decision-making, but consensus is too slow and inefficient for use with many agencies at once. Instead, the models in this layer work with a delegated or lead decision-maker.

Delegated or lead decision-making, although often more efficient than shared decision-making, risks the alienation, dissatisfaction, and reduced buy-in of other participants in the collaboration. Chen (2010) refers to this effect in terms of compromise of agency autonomy. Here, the history of New Zealand's public administration is important. Agencies are used to being highly autonomous, and at least since 1988 there has been comparatively less centralized rulemaking compared to other nations (Schick 2001). Any attempt to constrain this autonomy is viewed with suspicion. Hugh Oliver, lead advisor on the creation of the 'functional leadership' approach, described 'a system where chief executives are used to having the freedom to manage, and have a default position of reluctance' when it comes to giving up that control. New Zealand tried to manage this anti-centralization senti- ment by delegating leadership roles to line agencies rather than central agencies; the initial 'functional leads' were in the Ministry of Social Development (responsible for leading property management), the Ministry of Business, Innovation and Employment (responsible for procurement), and the Department of Internal Affairs (responsible for information and commu- nication technologies).

Individuals were designated as responsible for leading common functions or professional services across the public service. This was easiest when agencies themselves were calling out for help. The different models vary in terms of formality. Voluntary and informal models are useful when it is acceptable for some agencies to opt in or out of participating, when influence is tacit or indirect, or when the goal is to seek opportunities rather than to manage risk. More formal models are used when agencies want to be very clear about what the delegated leaders will provide when they are responsible for quasi-regulatory functions, or when the leader is performing critical tasks on behalf of other agencies. All models require a designated leader to influ- ence other agencies.

Many of these models were developed between 2009 and 2012 under the label 'functional leadership'; Hugh Oliver explained this was 'more a convenient grouping than a single model; each of the functional leads was very different to the others'. More than perhaps the first or third layers, the models in this section are 'ideal types' with examples demonstrating that most practices draw from several models at once. In its role as finance lead, the Treasury uses elements of the 'head of profession' model and elements of an 'internal regulator' model as the administering agency for the Public Finance Act. The procurement lead has elements of the core 'functional lead' model but also delivers some 'shared functions' in negotiating whole-of- government contracts. Hugh explained 'the Toolkit has been useful for building a shared language, so we know that we're talking about the same thing, but practices have been shaped by compromises, individual leaders, and political calculations, and have evolved over time.'

4.1 Agencies Functioning Separately

Functioning separately is the traditional and New Zealand-default approach to managing public administration problems (Table 10). It is most effective when agencies each have unique functions that relate to unique problems. Using the language of Paul Helm (mentioned earlier), this might be cases with something like 30 per cent commonality, but 70 per cent of requirements are unique to one agency. For a common function, like data sharing, it might make sense for an intelligence agency not to participate because their security requirements are very different. Similarly, some professions are much more relevant to some agencies over others, for example, with most teachers employed by the Ministry of Education.

In this model, agencies organize their own work as normal. They set their own processes, platforms, and internal policies and take responsibility for building the capability of their own employees. Funding is drawn from the agency's individual appropriation. There may be limited interoperability between the systems of one agency and other. This means that an individual moving from one role in one agency to a similar role in another agency will have a steep learning curve. Data sharing will be more difficult across different standards and platforms.

Agencies functioning separately means that a team in one agency may lack the critical mass to maintain the necessary capability to manage each function

Table 10 Agencies functioning separately model

Collaboration context	Costs of acting together outweigh the costs of acting alone
Problem type	Functions or problems are unique to a single agency
Planning and activity	Agencies organize their own work as normal
Agreement on goals and outcomes	Internal management decisions and budget bids for new items
Governance	Agency hierarchies and monitoring of major projects
Ministerial relationships	Separately to separate ministers
Incentives	Annual reporting and audit, ministerial accountability, and recognition for CEs
Funding	Individual agency appropriation

appropriately. This is exacerbated in small agencies where, for example, the procurement function might be completed by a single employee. That single employee is unlikely to be able to maintain knowledge and systems across the breadth of the procurement function to the same level that an aggregated team could do. Having thirty-five teams develop their own processes may be duplicative, and further inefficiencies may emerge from uneven workflows and difficulty managing surge capacity.

4.2 Voluntary Club

The voluntary club model is well suited to issues that are likely to be solved by the consistent application of good practice to particular functions of government (Table 11). Because it is self-organizing, this model works best when built off an existing grouping (e.g., professions or common job titles) that can be leveraged to share educational opportunities and foster discussion. Voluntary clubs can be used to share experiences of effective practice throughout professional networks that members then aspire to themselves. This model can also be used as a trial for more formal models if the full benefits are not realized.

Voluntary clubs are unlikely to receive much funding beyond minimal baseline funding from agencies. However, clubs that fund themselves may benefit from the resulting independence. The legitimacy of the club can be improved with the formal recognition of the Public Service Commissioner, validating the group's objectives as being in the interest of the public service collectively.

Table 11 Voluntary club model

Collaboration context	A self-identified group wants to work together, may be a natural professional network
Problem type	Improvements in consistency, capability, and professionalism
Planning and activity	Voluntary participation to build 'best practice'
Agreement on goals and outcomes	Objectives set by members
Governance	No formal governance, although a leader is usually selected by consensus and recognized by the Commissioner
Ministerial relationships	No direct role for ministers
Incentives	Normative pressures in the self-identified group
Funding	From baselines for specific activities

4.2.1 Case Study: Government Economics Network

The Government Economics Network (GEN) was established as an incorporated society in 2011 to act as a professional forum for development and networking, as well as to promote stronger linkages between economics and public policy, and improve economic advice to government.

The Network runs social and educational events like seminars and conferences to help achieve its objectives. Funding for the activities is limited, with the Network instead relying on members to volunteer their time, and charging for some of the events – especially its annual conference. Membership is not restricted to economists and is instead open to anyone interested in the application of economics to public policy. This voluntary component is in contrast to the Government Legal Network (GLN) (discussed further in the text), for which membership is dictated by profession.

GEN Chair Mark Lea observed that the UK Civil Service treats economists very differently – they form part of a recognized professional group, the Government Economic Service, and are managed centrally and deployed deliberately across the civil service. They tend to have job titles that include the word 'economics' or 'economist' in some way. In contrast, in New Zealand, there is frequently no one with that title in an agency, or perhaps a single 'Chief Economist'. People with various levels of economics training are employed in general policy roles, and many policy analysts are expected to use economic tools and theories in their analysis. These murky boundaries made economics more suited to an informal and voluntary club based on self-identification, and any public servant can join GEN if they want to build their capability in economic analysis.

GEN's status as an incorporated society placed it outside the government structure. This meant that it was not dependent on sponsorship from senior officials, but instead on the commitment of volunteer members. This is now becoming a limiting factor, as relying on volunteers is stopping GEN from pursuing all the objectives that its board would like to achieve. GEN is looking to move to a staffed model in order to grow and to expand their activities in promoting the relevance of economics to decision-makers.

4.3 Functional Leader/Head of Profession

The functional leadership/head of profession model offers a slightly stronger alternative to the voluntary club; activity is still primarily related to guidance and influence rather than standard-setting, but a clearer mandate is required to drive improvements (Table 12). It is most effective where agencies are unlikely to oppose guidance being set for their behaviour. These roles are typically

Table 12 Functional leader/Head of profession model

Collaboration context	An agency or public service leader has clear natural responsibility for improving a specific area of government performance, but giving them the power to direct other agencies is not appropriate
Problem type	Improvements relating to a demographic group or a function of government can be effected through influence, transparency, and so on
Planning and activity	A leader is designated responsibility for an area of government performance, leading across the system with support and commitment from core public service CEs
Agreement on goals and outcomes	Proposal to be revised and collectively agreed upon by a leadership team of core public service CEs
Governance	Leadership team of CEs hold each other collectively responsible in accordance with their agreements
Ministerial relationships	Either separate to the leader's own minister(s), balanced by collective agreements, or no ministerial relationship
Incentives	Voluntary guidelines set by leader, standards agreed by CEs, clear expectations among the CE group, normative pressure, recognition of good practice, reporting of performance information (either to the CEs, ministers and/or public), and recognition for CEs
Funding	Any combination of the leader funding activities from their baseline, club funding for collective-good activity, and/or system fund for cross-agency work

established by Cabinet, with individuals appointed by the Public Service Commissioner. The government may allocate a dedicated budget, and/or agencies may contribute funding by mutual agreement.

The leader is hosted within the agency that best matches its remit. Sometimes this is obvious, for example, the Solicitor-General is responsible for the legal profession. In other cases, there is no obvious match, and the leader is designated based on personal traits, for example, the chief executive of the Department of Corrections, Ray Smith, was designated as functional lead for health and safety; when Ray moved to the Ministry for Primary Industries, the responsibility for leadership of health and safety travelled with him. The functional leader is responsible to a minister for their function, who may or may not be the same minister as in the host department.

This model is best used to improve the delivery of a function or profession that is applicable across the system but that is not currently receiving adequate focus or support at senior levels. By demarcating responsibility for that functional area, it can also help alleviate pressure on other chief executives leading agencies. More than the voluntary club, this model is useful when the cohort of affected public servants is demarcated clearly. For example, GEN is a voluntary club in part because economics is not a recognized function or profession and instead people with economics knowledge are distributed across different teams. In contrast, the GLN is a functional leader/head of profession because legal advisors are a recognized and distinct group that tends to be part of dedicated legal teams within agencies.

4.3.1 Case Study: Government Legal Network

The GLN was created in 2011 to link all lawyers employed by public agencies (about 1,250 lawyers). The network is led by the Solicitor-General of the Crown Law Office as the head of the government legal profession and has a budget of approximately $1 m per year. The GLN offers professional mentoring, training, and knowledge sharing for the purpose of improving legal advice capability; 'in the past, one agency might have run a workshop exclusively for its own staff – now, increasingly, we share training resources' (past GLN Director Phil Griffiths, as quoted in State Services Commission 2017b).

Before the network's creation, legal practice across government agencies was seen to be inconsistent, exacerbated by variable sizes of legal teams (resulting from variably sized departments) and a lack of professional support between peers. Kevin Allan, Deputy Chief Executive of the Crown Law Office noted that GLN overcame the challenges of working in small agencies by operating 'as part of one professional community, [where] we combine our efforts' (State Services Commission 2017b).

Some other jurisdictions had addressed this problem with a more centralized approach where the Solicitor-General acts as the employer of all government lawyers. Instead, the GLN operates as a 'middle' solution that improves the quality and consistency of practice without the cost and disruption of centralization. In April 2016, Cabinet made the GLN a permanent responsibility of the Solicitor-General, which is an alternative to the approach of other jurisdictions, where the Solicitor-General formally employs government lawyers (more like the 'shared functions' model in the Toolkit). The GLN operates as a 'middle' solution that skirts the cost and disruption of the centralized approach while still addressing the consistency and quality of professional practice. As Chief Legal Advisor at Oranga Tamariki, Erin Judge notes, 'Having something like the GLN, which is able to coordinate different groups and share knowledge, is such a valuable resource' (GLN 2014).

4.4 System Leader

System leadership is used to standardize and improve activity across government that would benefit from a more consistent approach (Table 13). It is most usefully deployed in areas where functional leadership and softer solutions have not achieved the desired effect. The model assigns responsibility to an existing public service chief executive for providing leadership across the public service system for a particular area of activity.

This model builds on the functional leader/heads of profession by allowing the system leader to set standards that the other agencies are required to follow.

Table 13 System leader model

Collaboration context	Capability in a specific area is varied across agencies and less formal arrangements have not succeeded in improving or standardizing
Problem type	Stronger, more centralized coordination of certain functions is required to improve government performance; there are benefits to a common approach (e.g., standard-setting, infrastructure provisions, capability, strategic planning or investment, assurance)
Planning and activity	A public service leader or agency is mandated to lead on a particular function
Agreement on goals and outcomes	Agreed with minister and strategic direction set by leadership group of public service CEs
Governance	Leader keeps CE group updated, possibility of a CE governance group
Ministerial relationships	Direct to an appropriate minister for the function or agency
Incentives	As for functional leader/head of profession as well as possibility of assurance function and/or mandatory standards as approved by Cabinet
Funding	Any combination of the leader funding activities from their baseline, club funding for collective-good activity, and/or system fund for cross-agency work

Like the previous model, this model also establishes a direct line of account-ability to a minister without the necessity of delegation or legislation, and without the costly disruption of a whole new agency structure. These measures are used to manage tensions between individual agency interests and the cross-agency function targeted for improvement. System leaders are appointed by the Public Service Commissioner.

This model was intended to mitigate perceived loss of autonomy by working with the consent of chief executives. The idea was that chief executives would collectively agree to delegate certain responsibilities to a system leader to act on their behalf. Then, their agencies would follow through on this agreement by committing to implement the standard developed. In practice, the full and specific agreement of chief executives to delegate responsibility to a system leader has not yet been realized, and system leaders have operated with a mix of chief executive consent and Cabinet mandate.

4.4.1 Case Study: Government Chief Digital Officer

Strictly speaking, there are no in-practice examples of the 'system leader' model; however, the Government Chief Digital Officer (GCDO) is a close analogue. Originally established in 2012, the GCDO is responsible for improving the use of ICT. This role was established by Cabinet mandate in 2012 and delegated to the chief executive of the Department of Internal Affairs. Current GCDO, Paul James, observed that ICT is unique in being 'so central to agencies' core business models,' such that the nature of interagency collaboration needed to be a little different. In addition, 'for many agencies, [ICT is] the biggest item on their balance sheet – there are real fiscal pressures around replacing depreciating assets'. 'Soft', purely voluntary models were therefore insufficient to manage large investments, but 'hard' models were unsuitable because ICT could not be partitioned from the agencies' core services. Adding complexity, these agencies are led by chief executives who 'in most cases aren't digital natives – ICT is a real pressure point for them from a cost and performance perspective and they want help in understanding how it effects their business'.

In 2015 the GCDO set up what is now called the Digital Government Partnership, bringing together stakeholders from across government to support five strategic focus areas: leadership, technology, investment, information and digital services. The leadership group and five working groups that make up the partnership were intended to have an advisory role, rather than the governance role described in the System Leader model. Nonetheless, Paul has been very focused on orienting his team around the needs of agencies:

> I've seen collaborative leadership fail when the leaders get focused on telling people what they need. I spent a lot of time with my team to stress that our key customer is other agencies ... We ask: 'What are the systemic barriers to those agencies being successful, and how do we help remove some of those barriers?'

He describes this shift to thinking about enabling other agencies as 'hugely important, and something we're still evolving'. While ministerial support remains important, getting agency buy-in has reduced the need to rely on Cabinet mandate.

In the past couple of years, Paul has flipped the Digital Government Partnership agenda. Rather than start with what the GCDO is doing, the agenda now starts with chief executives describing their needs – 'It's really important to have a channel to hear what agencies are struggling with ... if you want to be a system lead, you need to start with system need.' The GCDO is currently helping agencies with cloud services adoption, digital identity, and a common process model for digital infrastructure. Paul was quick to note that a common process model did not mean a single system, but either multiple instances of the same systems or interoperability between systems:

> You need to be more sophisticated than thinking it's all the same or all bespoke. There might be some processes that are consistent across all agencies, and as agencies replace legacy assets, we support them with aligning those things that are pretty standard .... Then some processes you might see similar agencies using interoperable systems – one agency might look at [another] and think 'Our business is similar' .... Then there's the truly bespoke stuff.

4.5 Internal Regulator/Monitor

The internal regulator or monitor model is a well-established solution to problems that require strict adherence to rules, standards, and processes in matters of trust, confidence, and legitimacy (Table 14). In this way, it is much more specifically targeted than broader issues of improving performance of functions across agencies. It is a relatively 'hard' solution, in which one agency can direct other agencies and achieve compliance using a legislated mandate. Accordingly, the agency has a line of direct accountability to a minister and administers its own appropriation.

4.5.1 Case Study: The Treasury

The Treasury is a central government agency that provides oversight of the government financial system through monitoring, management, and the provision of advice on economic and fiscal policy. Its internal regulator role involves: authoring budget documents, monitoring imprest supply, producing monthly

Table 14 Internal regulator/monitor

Collaboration context	An agency has or requires a legislative mandate to direct other agencies
Problem type	Requires adherence to rules/standards/processes to uphold public trust and confidence (fiduciary responsibility rather than system performance improvement)
Planning and activity	Individual agency operates in accordance with its legislative framework to achieve compliance from other agencies
Agreement on goals and outcomes	Set out in a legislative framework
Governance	Individual agency
Ministerial relationships	Direct to minister responsible for agency
Incentives	Legislative authority to issue instruction to other agencies, ministerial direction, regulations
Funding	Individual agency appropriation

financial reports for audit, and maintaining an adequate 'system of internal control designed to provide reasonable assurance that the transactions recorded are within statutory authority' (The Treasury 2021).

Cabinet papers authored by other agencies that have financial implications are required to present specified financial information to obtain Treasury sign-off. Treasury also dictates deadlines and designs templates for budget proposals. The influence of the Treasury comes from several sources. Parliament establishes the rules through the Public Finance Act, which gives certain functions to the Treasury. Cabinet decisions have also created expectations that agencies engage with the Treasury in certain areas. Finally, there's informal influence, where agencies comply with Treasury 'guidance' on budget bids because they want to improve their chances of being successful in increasing their funding.

In Section 2, we noted that sometimes problems can be addressed by utilizing a combination of models from the Toolkit. In this case, Treasury has a regulatory function in administering the Public Finance Act, but since 2014 has also acted as the head of the finance profession. Government Chief Accountant Paul Helm leads a small team responsible for improving finance capability across the public service. He lacks the formal mandate of the GCDO, but instead works with influence, noting 'sometimes the lack of a mandate is a weakness, and sometimes it's a strength. A mandate comes with clear boundaries, whereas I can work much more informally – it's all about influencing'. Some of this influencing has been in helping to develop a new cadre of Chief Financial Officers (CFOs), where Paul sits on selection and interview panels, advises chief executives on their agency's performance, and works with senior finance professionals to provide them with the development opportunities needed to ascend to the CFO role.

Paul characterized the finance profession as operating somewhere between the dispersed economics profession and the demarcated legal profession: 'There are finance teams, but there's also accountants scattered around in other roles. For some things I go through the CFOs, but on others I've got an email list of 1500 people.'

The finance profession is partly funded by Treasury because they saw flow on benefits of improving finance capability for financial and budget management, but it also receives voluntary contributions from agencies who see value in the training courses that Paul's team provides.

4.6 Shared Functions

Shared functions is an alternative functional leadership model that is appropriate for capability or efficiency problems that could be addressed with centralization (Table 15). Functions that are complex or highly skilled but infrequent, or that have high levels of duplication, or where there are capability deficits in many agencies may benefit from a centralized approach. This is particularly valuable in New Zealand, given that the nation's public sector is made up of many small agencies that often have small functional teams. In this model, Cabinet assigns an agency responsible for providing a particular function on behalf of most or all other agencies. This reduces direct costs to individual agencies who no longer need to perform that function themselves. Therefore, funding is cost-recovery through fee for service, with fees periodically reviewed.

This is an appropriate approach when an individual agency can be identified as a centre of excellence for a given function, performing it more capably and efficiently than other agencies. Scale is an important consideration with which to weigh the possible benefits of centralized functions. Some larger departments may be more efficient working on their own rather than through a cross-agency approach, as they can achieve sufficient scale internally such that shifting to a shared functions model does not justify the additional transaction costs. A key consideration when applying a shared functions approach is whether the functional requirements are consistent or compatible across agencies. If different agencies have different requirements that cannot be reconciled, then a shared function may not provide significant efficiency advantages.

Table 15 Shared functions model

Collaboration context	An agency is identified as performing a function more capably or efficiently than other agencies with the same function
Problem type	Capability is concentrated in one agency; outcomes for other agencies are poor
Planning and activity	One agency assumes responsibility for performing or delivering a function on behalf of others
Agreement on goals and outcomes	By Cabinet at establishment of mandate, recognized by core public service CEs
Governance	Agency updates CE group, governance group of CEs may provide additional support
Ministerial relationships	Direct to appropriate minister assigned on establishment of mandate
Incentives	Incentives to encourage entrepreneurialism
Funding	Fee for service (cost-recovery), reviewed periodically

4.6.1 Case Study: Procurement Functional Lead

In 2009, the chief executive of the Ministry of Economic Development (now Ministry of Business, Innovation and Employment) was given leadership responsibility for Government Procurement to drive a step change in the performance of procurement functions. In part, it operated as a system lead, working with agencies to build capability, and setting standards for procurement. In other ways, it operated as a shared function model, engaging in whole-of-government negotiations with suppliers to get better procurement deals for agencies. This meant that it was performing these negotiations on behalf of and instead of those agencies, beginning with four contracts: stationery, vehicles, desktop and laptop computers, and multi-function printers.

Agencies were initially given the freedom to opt in to these whole-of-government negotiations, and some were reluctant to join. John Ivil ran the procurement function from 2009 until 2020 and progressively brought agencies on board by demonstrating the value that a shared approach could deliver: 'We weren't reducing their choice or their independence. The success was being seen as working with them, not against them.' When John's team was able to realise $140 million in savings from those first four contracts, more and more agencies chose to participate.

The model has resulted in several clear successes so far, securing New Zealand status as a leading nation ranked number 1 in the world at procurement

(Blavatnik School of Government 2019). By 2012, John had already 'exceeded goals of cost saved'. By the time he left the role in 2020, the model had 'realised over $1 billion just in hard savings'. Government contracts are benchmarked against market price, allowing them to identify direct cost avoidance. However, other benefits are less easy to measure: 'Better specification, better results, less or better-managed risk, capability building' and reduced complexity. Additionally, the current single procurement policy superseded the thirty-five policies operational at the time of the model's introduction, which made it easier for agencies to comply and for suppliers to engage with government.

However, in some ways the Procurement Functional Lead has been the victim of its own success. It now operates on a much larger scale, with up to 3,500 agencies involved. Beyond the thirty-five agencies of the public service, the Ministry of Business, Innovation and Employment now engages in negotiations on behalf of Crown entities, district health boards, schools, and many others. This makes their work of encouraging collaboration, building awareness of potential risks, and identifying opportunities for shared resourcing a lot harder. The process of making value propositions and setting up contracts now takes six months, where they used to take four months. The Procurement Functional Lead also now faces pressure to deliver public value on top of value for money, using procurement to achieve environmental and social outcomes. John sees some of the solutions to these problems as being greater investment in digitization to speed up delivery, and a greater profile for the work at a leadership level to improve understanding of the drivers of risk in significant service contracts.

5 Interagency Collaboration for Service Delivery

> Shared goals and trusted local relationships that come working together for longer periods of time is what sustains effective collaboration.
>
> *(Hugo Vitalis, lead advisor on many of New Zealand's place-based models)*

Citizens often must engage with multiple government agencies around a single problem or life event. Sometimes this is just an inconvenience – having to provide the same information multiple times or having to queue in multiple lines. Other times it's also inefficient for government – double-handling reducing the cost-effectiveness of service delivery. For individuals and families with high/complex needs, sometimes the only way to make a lasting change is through multiple service providers working together with these individuals and families towards a single bespoke plan.

This section deals with models for addressing shared service delivery problems at the frontline and in communities (Table 16). These solutions orient services around users and places. Unlike centrally designed policy or

Table 16 Models for organizing around public service delivery

Non-collaborative	Softer				Harder
Agencies delivering separately	Co-location	Collective impact network	Collective impact board	Federated services	Delivery vehicles

administrative solutions that may be amenable to top-down design, frontline service collaboration examples in the Toolkit often involve local entrepreneurs working from the bottom-up. This means there tends to be a proliferation of different solutions in different parts of the country. The purpose of the Toolkit in these situations is not to standardize a recommended set of approaches, but to provide archetypal starting points such that practitioners are not beginning with a blank page.

An earlier study on collaboration in the New Zealand public service (Eppel et al. 2014) noted that these frontline entrepreneurs were most effective when protected from interference by a 'guardian angel'. This is not necessarily because the entrepreneurs were working outside the rules, but that attention brought formal processes that were too rigid to allow for rapid and iterative solutions. Making these models work requires delegating decision-making closer to the service interface, and national hierarchies being more comfortable with variation. Hugo Vitalis, Manager of Strategy and Innovation at the Public Service Commission, noted a tension in sharing local solutions: 'The concern is that if we shine too bright a light on what these people are doing, they get caught up in all the processes and the innovation will be squashed.'

At the 'softest' end, the project team observed that some types of problems had been improved simply by better knowledge sharing between agencies. While public administration literature on the effectiveness of co-location arrangements is mixed, there seems to be general acceptance that it can support tacit knowledge exchange (Hagebak 1979; Agranoff 1991; Jennings and Krane 1994; Lee et al. 2009; O'Flynn et al. 2011; Memon and Kinder 2017). As the need for coordination increases, the team concluded that tacit knowledge exchange needed to be augmented by shared planning (Collective Impact Network model) and shared prioritization (Collective Impact Board model).

Much of this layer is informed by literature on delivery networks, used to make sense of observations of New Zealand practice. Hugo reports being directly influenced by the works of Agranoff (2004) and Provan and Kenis (2008), as well as the 'collective impact' model described by Kania and Kramer (2011). Networks can provide innovative solutions to complex problems, but sometimes these solutions are just too messy to be efficient, consistent, and fair, or provide confidence that there are no gaps or omissions (Davies 2002, 2012). When resources can be clearly identified, it may be possible to achieve alignment and reduce double-handling through shifting responsibilities. The two 'harder' models in this layer of the Toolkit involve one agency delivering services on behalf of another. This might be as simple as one agency collecting information on behalf of other agencies and sharing it with them with the individuals' consent. Or it could be the more complex creation of a 'joint-venture' that allows multiple agencies to pool resources and deliver services together.

There is a difference in appropriate performance management methods from softer models to harder models. Ouchi (1979) described networks that achieve through goal alignment, something we see in the softer models, and contrasted these with contracts that achieve through performance specification, as seen in 'Federated Services' and 'Delivery Vehicle' models. A similar distinction was observed by Chen (2010), who distinguished between bottom-up goal-alignment and top-down mandated solutions.

Models in this layer differ from the other layers in the Toolkit in that they may consider the involvement of local government and NGOs. Like many governments, New Zealand has contracted the provision of many services to other organizations, and effective service coordination necessarily involves these organizations as well. Cross-sectoral collaboration is the subject of a much broader set of literature, and this Element only considers these from the perspective of the central government.

5.1 Agencies Delivering Separately

Delivering separately1 constitutes the traditional approach to managing service delivery (Table 17). It is effective in cases where services fall clearly within the responsibility of single agencies, and these divisions are easily navigable by users without assistance. Its operating processes and structures are as familiar for service delivery as they are for administration and policy. Agencies agree on goals and outcomes through their usual internal programmes, delivering their services separately from other agencies, funded by their individual appropriations and sometimes contracting out to other organizations. They are governed through typical agency hierarchies, with an individual ministerial relationship at the top. Professional values and standards provide the necessary incentives for participation in this model.

Table 17 Agencies delivering separately model

Collaboration context	History of successful single-agency working
Problem type	Low overlap between services, easy for users to navigate on their own
Planning and activity	Agencies pursuing normal priorities and running their own services
Agreement on goals and outcomes	As normal and with professional practice to recognize overlaps, make referrals and manage complex cases
Governance	Agency hierarchies, possibility of contracting for service provision
Ministerial relationships	Separately to separate ministers
Incentives	Professional values and standards
Funding	Single-agency appropriations, direct delivery or contracting to a third party

5.2 Co-location

By co-locating (Table 18), public servants can engage in tacit knowledge sharing and informal meetings, gaining a better understanding of each other's work and recognizing opportunities to work together. Typically, one agency will hold a commercial lease, and other agencies will effectively sub-let space from them and pay a contribution towards shared costs. They may share meeting rooms, cafeteria space, reception services, printers, or other amenities. Agency teams may all sit together or may intermingle with public servants from other agencies, particularly in a 'hot-desk' environment where individuals may move desks and sit close to each other based on specific projects.

These simple conveniences were observed to lead to spontaneous conversations, information sharing, and cross-pollination of ideas. Co-located teams, sometimes put together simply out of geographic proximity, inevitably led to collaborative projects even when none had previously existed. Co-located teams can form new shared social identities related to that office location, further encouraging future collaboration.

While co-location is not necessarily sufficient for overcoming agency boundaries, it has been observed as a stepping stone on the way to more structured models of collaborative service delivery. It can allow agencies to investigate the extent of possible overlaps in service delivery and how these could be reduced to improve both user experience and efficiency. It can be a useful preliminary

Table 18 Co-location model

Collaboration context	Agencies have identified opportunities for greater alignment
Problem type	Improvements needed in tacit knowledge sharing and relationships, or potential overlaps
Planning and activity	Co-located offices or staff on local teams
Agreement on goals and outcomes	Voluntary by participating agencies, working with procurement functional lead and external partners (e.g., local government, NGOs) where appropriate
Governance	Self-governing, or a location manager provided by participating agency
Ministerial relationships	Separately to separate ministers, or to a place-based portfolio as appropriate
Incentives	Encouragement from public service leaders and ministers
Funding	Any combination of shared costs, shared administration, or varying agency contributions (e.g., location manager)

step to building collaborative capacity (Bardach 1998) because it requires agencies to balance their interests, even if only with respect to accommodation issues.

5.2.1 Case Study: Auckland Policy Office

The Auckland Policy Office (APO) is a co-location arrangement that brings together government agencies to focus on the challenges and opportunities facing Auckland. Auckland is recognized as the social and economic centre of a rapidly changing New Zealand, whose potential the public service needs to play a part in realizing. Having a stronger local presence and a deeper understanding of the needs and challenges of the city is a first step.

In this way, the APO identifies and develops local policies, promotes central government involvement in regional development, and acts as a source of information about Auckland. In addition to the cost-saving benefits of co-location, the office acts as a hub that builds a cross-agency view of Auckland's policy issues, enabling collaboration and strengthening coordination between central government agencies and key Auckland stakeholders, including Auckland Council and its associated agencies. It also provides opportunities for data and evidence sharing, and risk evaluation, management, and escalation.

In 2005, the APO was set up and nominally led by the then Ministry of Economic Development, before being transferred to the Public Service Commission in 2015. Lewis Holden worked on the initial setup and subsequently became the inaugural Deputy Commissioner for Auckland (a role within the Public Service Commission) with responsibility for leading the APO. Lewis commented that 'much of my career has been trying to do cross-agency collaboration'.

Despite this leadership role, participation is voluntary, and agencies involved in the APO retain management responsibility for their own staff. This calls for a softer governance structure in which agencies that do choose to participate sign a Memorandum of Understanding with the lead agency that outlines broad requirements for the office's operations. A 'body corporate' style mechanism enhances consultation with participating agencies on the office's strategic development and ongoing operation. A leadership team of senior representatives further supports collaboration across the seventeen-member agencies, albeit without formal accountability mechanisms or reporting lines between agency leads or ministers.

The accountability structure does inhibit some of the more ambitious collaborative goals of the Office – participating agencies originally agreed to free up 10 per cent of their staff time to focus on cross-agency work, but the enduring accountability lines between staff and their managers in Wellington limited that possibility in practice. Lewis has championed collaborative work, even if a staff member's participation in the collective was limited to the social club committee, noting that it keeps the staff from different agencies talking to each other.

The voluntary nature of the APO means that it requires a strong value proposition to attract participants. Such benefits are the efficiencies and savings; central site within Auckland; linkages with other agencies, Auckland Council and other local stakeholders; and the potential to host ministers working out of Auckland. 'There's a huge amount of tacit knowledge exchange' said Lewis, 'even though our attempts to get true collaboration and a real team-based approach has only been partially or sporadically successful'. Lewis described the importance of 'regular stand-up meetings' where agencies shared what they were working on, and 'water cooler conversations'. The information sharing was so strong that Lewis observed: 'We often had staff from Wellington come up and comment that in one day at the APO they found out more about what other Wellington-based agencies were doing than they could while based permanently in Wellington.'

Lewis believed that there were two possible paths to growing the effectiveness of the APO – the development of more structured collaborative governance mechanisms (like the models discussed in sections 5.3 and 5.4) around specific problems, or a senior minister who championed a more integrated approach to managing Auckland place-based issues. A specific Auckland focus was needed because:

> Public servants in Wellington don't always understand Auckland. Most of the issues we [New Zealanders] have to grapple with, Auckland has to grapple with first. Whether it was transport congestion, multiculturalism, or housing affordability – it tends to hit Auckland first and if you can solve it there it's instructive for the rest of the country.

5.3 Collective Impact Network

Some individuals and families have complex needs that do not neatly fit with existing service offerings. When families face a combination of physical and mental health problems, addiction, disability, access to education, poverty, homelessness, and crime, these problems tend to be among the most intractable. Because the problems are complex, the required solutions are often bespoke. New Zealand has trialled a variety of collaborative models to address these kinds of problems, all involving the clustering of service providers and the agreement of the individual or family to an integrated plan (Table 19).

The coordination of wraparound support is typically time-consuming and cannot be sustained at a population-wide level. A group of agencies will agree to the prioritization of a small group of individuals or families on which they will focus their attention. These individual cases will be identified by frontline professionals based on their need and willingness to engage in an intensive intervention to simultaneously address multiple challenges. The individuals or families will be invited to participate in a workshop with those professionals who they would like to work with, and the client and professionals will agree to a plan. In the simpler or less-formalized networks, a service professional who is trusted by the client will take responsibility for coordinating and monitoring the delivery of services in accordance with the plan, as well as reconvening the group as needed to check on progress and adapt the plan over time. In more difficult cases, a network administrator will be required to coordinate action, broker services, and report progress. Information sharing across the network can be strengthened by combining elements of the co-location model, although there may also be privacy considerations that require innovative solutions.

This model does not involve moving any functions or services between agencies, relying instead on leadership through influence and accessing

Table 19 Collective impact network model

Collaboration context	Resources and services used by a common group are dispersed across a number of agencies that have the capability and leadership to wrap around users without aggregating to one agency
Problem type	Users are unable to navigate and coordinate the services they need, a small enough number of cases can be identified, a range of services needs to be tailored to unpredictable and/or highly individualized needs
Planning and activity	A network of agencies (and NGOs) agrees to a specific work programme to provide wraparound services to a shared group
Agreement on goals and outcomes	Determined nationally through ministerial priorities and budget processes, locally by a collective impact board, or mutually with those affected, supported by national-level data and targeting
Governance	Practitioners determining action plan through regular meetings and updates and/or by a network administrator
Ministerial relationships	Separately to separate ministers, or to a place-based portfolio as appropriate
Incentives	Professional values, intrinsic motivation, and mutual commitments (made by practitioners and individual/family)
Funding	Network administrator and/or service broker funded by board (test and learn) or individualized budgets

existing capability distributed among the agencies. The main incentive for participation by professionals is the intrinsic motivation to help the people they work with. Because of this, participation is not limited to central government, and networks have involved professionals from local government and NGOs.

These networks can be supported by dedicated backbone funding and champions higher up the hierarchy who can help remove bureaucratic barriers that would otherwise impede the delivery of the plan. In some cases, ministerial or chief executive attention has provided frontline professionals with the armour to defend themselves against claims from middle-managers that they are working outside their typical service mandate.

5.3.1 Case Study: Children's Teams

The following example describes the operation of Children's Teams as a network from 2012 to 2017. After this, the Children's Teams were shifted to a 'harder' model and fell under the formalized leadership of the Ministry for Children (Oranga Tamariki).

Children's Teams bring service providers from iwi (tribal authorities) and a range of sectors together to support at-risk children by making a single plan strengthened by input from a range of agencies across health, justice, education, and the wider social sector. The team approach developed in recognition that many at-risk children and their families have complex needs and require joined-up support that cannot be provided by any single agency. Teachers, social workers, nurses, and many other professionals have chosen these careers out of a desire to make a positive difference for the children they are working with. While not without tensions, the teams are motivated to work together because they recognize that this is the best way to help these children and their families. Hugo Vitalis, who designed several of New Zealand's place-based initiatives and interviewed Children's Teams around the country, was adamant that this sense of mission was stronger than any extrinsic incentive: 'They see Wellington (central government) as a drag on progress but maintain a hope that it might be an enabler – what they want to do is help the families they see every day, and what they need is the freedom to do it.' Hugo saw professions as having a strong role to play in a more delegated approach to service management, with professional values and norms helping those at the front line know the right thing to do, and related this to the 'clan'-based performance management described by Ouchi (1979).

The teams are focused on cross-agency working and information sharing in order to minimize duplication. They require prioritization of existing services and resources as well as empowerment for new ways of working. Practitioners and professionals from across a range of sectors work together alongside families, putting the needs of children first and sharing responsibility. At a practical level, the teams build those capabilities within the children's workforce to shift their emphasis. They set goals collaboratively with individuals and families to form a plan that all parties are equally committed to. The plans are also informed by national priorities for the sector, with target groups established by a board of representatives from health and social sector agencies.

For each child in the programme identified as needing wraparound support, a 'lead professional' is assigned to take a coordinating role across the other agencies involved. This lead professional is based on each child's needs and existing relationships, and on the family's preference. Each agency must make its staff available to act as lead professionals and do not receive additional funding for this. This funding arrangement differs from a similar programme, 'Family Partnership', in which the Ministry for Social Development administered a central fund that was used to support agencies and community organizations to back-fill staff time consumed by the lead professional role. Hugo noted that Children's Teams were heavily dependent on lead officials:

> Some of these leaders were real entrepreneurs – they were just relentless in looking for different ways to help. And when they reached out to others, they were often successful in accessing resources and capability that wasn't traditionally available. One family said that access to nutritious food was a barrier to them improving their health. They therefore wanted to grow their own vegetables but had no way to get started. The director of the children's team spoke with the manager at Bunnings (a hardware store) who donated all the materials needed for a vegetable garden.

Relying on the heroic actions of lead professionals was not without risk. Heroes are hard to find, and if those individuals were unavailable, or moved on, it was harder to sustain progress. In 2017, the Children's Teams models were changed so that network administrators could be funded and provided through a single organization – the Ministry for Children (Oranga Tamariki).

5.4 Collective Impact Board

While networks can be effective in situations where resources and capability are already available, sometimes more formalized governance arrangements are needed to make important trade-off decisions to reallocate resources towards higher priority activities. In this situation, New Zealand uses a governance board of regional leaders (Table 20) from participating agencies and organizations (possibly including those from outside government).

The model assigns collective responsibility to the board through Cabinet mandate for performance relating to local priorities. This process will also involve specifying the location boundaries of the mandate, agreeing the broad remit of activities in line with priorities at the national level, and assigning a lead minister to which the board will collectively report. The board is then responsible for agreeing to its collective local priorities by consensus. These will most usefully be specified as a small number of discrete results that are also associated with agreed measures. Ideally, the boards will organize themselves, although an independent chair may be necessary in some situations. To enable self-organization, chief executives of agencies represented on the board will need to collectively agree to consistent levels of delegation for decision-making to the members of the board.

Table 20 Collective impact board model

Collaboration context	Cabinet mandate required to sustain collaboration due to difficult trade-offs between priorities and/or local needs differs significantly from national priorities
Problem type	As for collective impact network – services difficult to navigate or aggregate
Planning and activity	Cabinet-mandated board of regional leaders has collective responsibility for performance relating to local priorities
Agreement on goals and outcomes	Set nationally for the overall remit, along with location boundaries. Interorganizational priorities determined locally by board consensus as a small number of discrete measurable results
Governance	Collective agreement of participating leaders to consistent delegations, board may use an independent chair but is ideally self-organizing
Ministerial relationships	Collectively to a lead minister as mandated by Cabinet
Incentives	Collective responsibility for improvements, supported by periodic reporting to and engagement with the local community
Funding	National- or collective-level agreement to pool funding for local priorities (agency contributions from baseline) and/or separate appropriation for local priorities

Funding for the board and its activities will be through national- or collective-level agreement to pool funding (i.e., contributions from agency baselines). Where the political will is high, it may also be possible to allocate a separate appropriation for local priorities. Incentives for the model are provided by the collective responsibility mechanism, strengthened by engagement with the local community that involves reporting back to them on progress.

5.4.1 Case Study: South Auckland Social Wellbeing Board

The South Auckland Social Wellbeing Board (originally called the South Auckland Social Investment Board) was established to focus on improving outcomes specifically for children and young people in the region of South Auckland.

The Board has a line of collective accountability to the lead minister (in this case, the Minister of Social Development) that runs through an independent chair. The lead minister is responsible for setting the overall direction of the model. Governance and local decision-making are then handled by the Board through consensus, which is made up of senior officials from eleven national-level agencies (but who are local to the area), and two local agencies, with an independent chair: Accident Compensation Corporation, Department of Corrections, Ministry of Education, Ministry of Health, Ministry of Justice, Ministry for Pacific Peoples, Ministry of Social Development, New Zealand Police, Kāinga Ora (Homes and Communities Agency), Oranga Tamariki (Ministry for Children), Te Puni Kōkiri (Ministry of Māori Development), Counties Manukau District Health Board, and the Southern Initiative (a division of Auckland Council that focuses on well-being in South Auckland).

The Public Service Commissioner consults with member agencies and the chair in order to make the Board appointments. Seniority of the local officials is a prerequisite that better enables them to influence programmes and services outside the direct remit of the Board. One Board member commented (as reported in Litmus 2019): 'We had to have all the relevant agencies around the table, but [we also] had to have the right people around the table. People who actually had the power to make a decision and then enact it.'

The lead minister appoints the chair of the Board in consultation with the Cabinet Appointment and Honours Committee. The role is a non-voting position intended to guide the decision-making process towards consensus while ensuring the accountability of members for their agencies' contributions to shared goals. The chair is also expected to front the Board's advice to Ministers and Members of Parliament as required. Participating agencies believed it was important that the chair was independent of those agencies, and also connected to the local community: 'She understands the mandate and the operations of many, if not all, of the agencies sitting around the table, but she is not of them. She is from the South Auckland community so is a credible player' (Litmus 2019).

The Board developed a plan for how support for children and young people in the area would be prioritized, coordinated, and delivered. This involved the reallocation of existing funds already used by agencies for service provision, supplemented by a small discretionary fund. While individual agencies continue to be accountable for the services they provide, the Board is accountable for the collective impact of these services. The South Auckland Social Wellbeing Board reports quarterly to the national-level Social Wellbeing Board against the agreed plan.

Despite the more formalized structure for reporting and accountability, one Board member reflected that progress still depended heavily on interpersonal relationships and trust: 'I think people have got to meet together on a regular basis, more regularly so that they start to develop decent trust with each other. Not sending stand-ins. Having room for opening the discussions, where they really start to understand each other, and understand each other's needs' (Litmus 2019).

5.5 Federated Services

When soft models are insufficient, some services are integrated differently, with one agency delivering services on behalf of others (Table 21). Earlier study by the Department of Internal Affairs revealed that New Zealanders can generally access individual services, but find it more difficult to access services from multiple agencies during certain life events such as the birth of a child or first enrolment in tertiary education (Cordes 2015). Businesses face similar challenges, with several agencies involved in registering a company or facilitating

Table 21 Federated services model

Collaboration context	Opportunity for improvements in grouping of services across and within agencies
Problem type	Users frustrated with existing arrangements, capability and economy of delivery could be improved, and/or services can be easily separated and transferred from one agency to another
Planning and activity	Services (including funding) transferred to another agency with related services that could be better delivered in combination
Agreement on goals and outcomes	Can be determined by entrepreneurial staff proposals, research to determine problem areas, or priorities and sequence agreed upon by group of core public service leaders
Governance	Appointed lead agency, service-level agreements with other agencies,
Ministerial relationships	Separately to separate ministers
Incentives	Primarily reporting – of pain points and progress/ successes to public service leaders and ministers
Funding	Transferred to lead agency, may also require a joint-venture vehicle to hold shared assets

international trade. Service Federation helps overcome some of these problems by having a single point of contact with citizens during a particular life event or business stage. Because these events are often stressful, making it easier to deal with government at these times has an outsized effect on citizens' and businesses' experience of government.

The services that are most suited to federation have a few common characteristics. One is that there is a clear lead agency that forms the contact point for almost everyone going through that life event. If there is no natural lead, federation is likely to have fewer benefits because citizens may need to be first directed by another agency to contact the lead agency. A second characteristic is that the services to be federated need to be simple and transactional. For example, a lead agency can collect or share information on behalf of another agency but may not be able to provide detailed professional care. When the services are deeper or more individualized, the Delivery Vehicles model may be more suitable.

Transfer of relevant resources comes with a transfer of accountability to the lead department, making the chief executive of that agency accountable to the relevant minister for the delivery of the federated services that cross-agency boundaries. Chief executives of other contributing agencies will likely retain only residual accountability depending on the scale of the resource transfer (see Figure 6). One of the key challenges of this model is that the full transfer of resources out of agencies can limit their buy-in and commitment to the shared goal.

5.5.1 Case Study: SmartStart

The SmartStart initiative allows parents to register the birth of a child with only one agency – the Department of Internal Affairs (DIA). This single interface

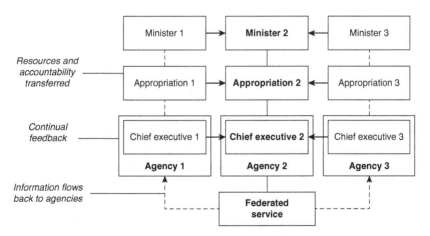

Figure 6 Federated services governance structure

allows parents to register their child for a National Health Index number to access health services, update any benefit entitlements and applications for parental support with the Ministry of Social Development, request a tax number for their child from the Inland Revenue Department, and receive information about several further services from parental support with mental health or budgeting, through to education options for the child.

DIA was a logical lead agency to administer the portal because all births must be registered with this agency to obtain a birth certificate. Jeff Montgomery, the Registrar-General of Births, Deaths and Marriages reported that 'It's now so much easier for parents to get the services and support they need to set up their child for the future' (State Services Commission 2017a).

The portal reduces the need to deal with multiple agencies and repeatedly provide the same information, directly addressing the finding from an earlier study that New Zealanders were frustrated at having to join-up government services themselves, switching between several agencies and providing the same information each time. Because SmartStart is delivered digitally, all transactions can be completed from anywhere, any time.

As well as the several government agencies, SmartStart also involves NGOs like the College of Midwives and Plunket (the major supplier of child wellness services). Karen Guilliland, Chief Executive of the College of Midwives at the time, gives evidence of the programme's success on several levels. Firstly, families the College works with have felt 'supported . . . to manage what can be confusing administrative processes with ease,' while the midwives themselves have had their work made easier with a 'single place to refer new parents to for a range of information' (State Services Commission 2017a).

Despite seeming like a purely technical solution, SmartStart relied heavily on the intrinsic motivation of employees at the participating agencies and organizations to make life easier for parents. Agencies needed to be willing to give up control and resources in order to shift service provision to the DIA. Plunket Chief Operative Officer Lois van Waardenberg noted that the progress of the model was thanks in large part to 'people and parts of our system prepared to prioritize our customers or citizens over parochial and more individual concerns' (State Services Commission 2017a). SmartStart also benefitted from championing at senior levels – it was encouraged by Ministers (Hipkins 2019c) and highlighted in national and public-facing reporting as part of the Better Public Service Results programme (Scott and Boyd 2022).

Some agencies were concerned that SmartStart would not provide them with the information about the child that they needed. This was addressed partially through secondments and co-location of staff from each affected agency into the DIA during the establishment of the SmartStart portal. Additionally, an advisory board was established so that agencies could raise any concerns with the chief executive of the DIA. This advisory board will likely be of continued importance as SmartStart expands and incorporates a variety of services – affected agencies will be keen to make sure their ongoing needs are not overlooked during this expansion.

5.6 Delivery Vehicles

The 'hardest' model envisaged in this layer of the Toolkit was the creation of a dedicated workforce to deliver integrated services on behalf of two or more agencies (Table 22). Legislation was amended in 2020 to allow two or more agencies to create a joint venture, effectively a new agency that is jointly 'owned' and governed by its parent agencies. Following agreement by Cabinet, this Delivery Vehicle can employ staff, own assets, and is accountable to a board consisting of the chief executives of the parent agencies. This accountability arrangement is important in ensuring that the Delivery Vehicle delivers the services that the parent agencies need, that contribute to the policy

Table 22 Delivery vehicles model

Collaboration context	Only core public service agencies are involved (as opposed to other organizations such as district health boards), services can be easily separated and transferred
Problem type	Service provision is the most important way to organize agencies; justifies significant disruption, upfront costs and potential exit costs
Planning and activity	Relevant services are located in a particular agency (possibly a new vehicle) to get best joined-up service delivery
Agreement on goals and outcomes	Cabinet decision or order in council
Governance	May be an agency or a sub-agency structure, or a joint venture governed accordingly
Ministerial relationships	Usually separately to separate ministers
Incentives	Annual reporting and audit under the Public Finance Act, ministerial accountability, and recognition for CEs
Funding	Individual appropriation

outcomes for which they are responsible, and that work in an integrated and coordinated way with other services delivered by that agency.

Joint ventures are well known and understood in the private sector as a means for reducing transaction costs, pooling resources, or maintaining options (Vitalis and Scott 2015). The statutory Delivery Vehicle was only made possible by legislation coming into effect in August 2020, and so there are no examples of this model in action.

However, the project team was inspired by several similar experiences that worked around legislative barriers. Public service departments were not previously able to enter into Delivery Vehicle arrangements because they are administrative divisions within the legal Crown, and two parts of the same legal entity cannot enter into contracts with each other. The Ministry of Foreign Affairs and Trade (MFAT) and New Zealand Trade and Enterprise (NZTE) had operated a joint venture called 'G2 G' (government-to-government) since 2014, which was possible because NZTE is an arms-length body legally separate from the Crown. G2 G was established to support New Zealand agencies to engage in commercial arrangements with other countries to leverage their expertise and knowledge. MFAT is responsible for New Zealand's foreign affairs and trade objectives, and NZTE brought commercial know-how.

Another example of structural solutions used to create an integrated work-force is the New Zealand Customs Services. Customs acts at the border, inspecting incoming goods to collect import duties and prevent the import of prohibited items. It makes operational sense for Customs to do both functions, as both require the agency to know who is importing what goods, and to have physical access to those goods to verify the contents of consignments. However, from a policy perspective, the two functions are not closely related. Customs collects import duties as part of New Zealand's taxation system. Prohibited items are detected and prevented from entering the country as part of New Zealand's system of law and order. Customs can therefore be conceived as delivering on the policy objectives of the taxation agency (Inland Revenue Department) and the police. Rather than being a joint venture of these agencies, Customs is an agency in its own right with its own budget, minister, and statutory reporting obligations.

These and other examples of service integration prompted the New Zealand government to amend the Public Service Act to enable the creation of Delivery Vehicles where agencies can directly engage with each other to create jointly governed agencies to deliver services on their behalf. This governance arrangement provides the parent agencies with greater control than equivalent participating agencies in the federated services model, and therefore is useful when principal-agent problems would otherwise be too great to allow service integration.

6 Conclusion

> The Toolkit doesn't have all the answers, but it's always the first place we look.
> *(Callum Butler, Principal Policy Advisor)*

Collaboration between government agencies remains a necessary part of contemporary public administration and a new normal of public servant life. It is not easy, but agencies continue to try to work together because they must: complex policy areas require integrated planning and prioritization across agencies; common functions and professions need leadership in order to build capability, interoperability, and resilience; and frontline services must be coordinated and integrated to better meet the needs of individuals, families, and businesses.

While collaboration literature has made significant strides in unpacking the black box of socio-technical processes that contribute to agencies working (or not working) together, this literature (as a whole) aims to reveal generalizable truths that make working across agency boundaries easier. Against this general landscape, several studies seek to unpack where certain practices might be more or less useful or applicable. Others call for more study to develop a contingent approach or dimensional framework, for more discriminant application of solutions to their contexts.

Collaboration literature acknowledges that practice is often ahead of theory. This Element explores practice across one national jurisdiction, where the New Zealand public service has applied a reasonably sophisticated contingency approach to the matching of collaborative models with problem contexts. The Toolkit described here was generated inductively by a group of senior public servants, based on observations and interactions with dozens of examples of interagency collaboration from 2004 until 2020. Those public servants also report being influenced by key readings in public administration literature. The axes or dimensions of the Toolkit are the problem type (policy, administration, service delivery), and the level of trade-off required against individual agency priorities. These axes were based on observations of how past examples clustered into similar types of working, or reflections from practitioners about what worked, when, and why.

6.1 Some Common Solutions

This Element is premised on the argument that interagency collaboration is not one thing, and that distinct contingent solutions are required for different problem contexts. But that is not to say that there is no commonality across and between the different models in the Toolkit, something acknowledged in the Toolkit guidance itself.

The Toolkit guidance identifies three technical elements that are likely to be useful across many of the different collaborative models: terms of reference, secretariats, and cascading levels of governance. It may seem obvious, but several of the examples discussed by the project team had either failed or floundered for a time because of the absence of a clear statement of the purpose, expectations, and processes of the collaboration. This could be overcome by something as simple as terms of reference document, or as involved as a procedural manual.

A common feature across many of the models is that collaboration needs administrative support. This is recognized across the literature of related fields, described as 'network administrative organisations' (Provan and Kenis 2008 or 'backbone organisations' (Kania and Kramer 2011). In New Zealand these tend to be called 'secretariats' and perform functions like organizing and preparing material for meetings, communicating decisions, and contributing to policy development.

Secretariats are often needed to support cascading levels of governance (Hanleybrown et al. 2012; Carey and Crammond 2015). Guidance relating to the Toolkit suggests that interagency collaboration benefits from the attention and signalling effect of chief executive involvement, often in the form of a high-level steering group that meets infrequently to set overall strategy. But chief executives do not do all the work themselves, nor can they assume that teams underneath them will automatically be aligned with teams in other agencies. A general feature of many of the models is interagency groups (decision-making groups, technical advisory groups, etc.) at various hierarchical levels through the respective agencies, each with a clear function and mandate.

6.1.1 Social, Not Just Technical

As noted in Section 1, psychological, behavioural, and social disposition of actors is likely to be a key determinant of collaborative success. It is by now a cliché to describe collaboration as an 'unnatural act between non-consenting adults' (Wuichet 2000, p. 67). This saying is perhaps reflective of selfish and individual conceptions of human behaviour that have risen and fallen in popularity across a range of disciplines – from Mill's 'economic man' (in Ingram 1888) to Dawkins' 'selfish gene' (1981). The team that worked on the Toolkit certainly observed behaviour that was based on individual interests and incentives, but also saw much that was prosocial and altruistic, closely reflecting the literature described in Section 1. Further, these prosocial behaviours were integral to those examples that were most successful. As Ross Boyd reported, 'the single most important factor was that people cared about making a difference'.

A key companion to the Toolkit is the New Zealand government's efforts to reflect increasingly humanistic conceptions of public servants (Scott and Macaulay 2020; Hughes and Scott 2021) and deliberate promotion of prosocial motivations and behaviours. In the most successful examples, the team that developed the Toolkit saw public servants applying discretionary effort and sacrificing their own objectives in favour of collaborative goals where they believed that this would result in better outcomes for New Zealanders. The New Zealand public service has emphasized public service motivation under the label 'a spirit of service to the community', with new legislative requirements for chief executives to take action to 'preserve, protect and nurture the spirit of service ... that public service employees bring to their work' (Public Service Act 2020, s. 13; Scott and Macaulay 2020, p. 579).

The team also observed that collaboration was most successful when public servants understood the purpose or goal of the work, judged this goal worthwhile, felt that their actions were instrumental in achieving that goal, and believed that others would sustain effort towards the goal for long enough for the collaboration to be successful. Ross Boyd saw goal commitment as a key success indicator: 'Collaboration is never easy, but some people persisted, despite the setbacks.'

There has also been a renewed push to encourage a social identity as 'public servants' that spans agency boundaries. Prior to the 1980s, the New Zealand public service was largely self-conceived as a single service with a single employer; later, public servants were employed by individual agencies, and chief executives cultivated distinct agency cultures (Scott 2019). Recent reforms in New Zealand have aimed to create a 'unified public service' (Hipkins 2019b, p. 1) based around a shared identity, through shared symbols and signifiers, with the intention of creating more collaborative behaviour. Callum Butler observed that: 'You can get more done when there's a feeling you're on one team.'

Also reflecting the collaboration literature described in Section 1, trust was observed as a key enabler. The Justice Sector was an example of collaboration that was sustained from 2004 until the present, and participants pointed to relationships and following through on procedural commitments as key components. Aphra Green, Justice Sector Group Manager, observed 'a lot of it is meeting together, week after week, and building that trust'.

While unnecessary meetings clearly introduce additional transaction costs to collaboration, many interviewees emphasized the value of investing time in building relationships.

As senior public servants move from role to role, longer-term collaborative arrangements need to survive beyond any specific interpersonal arrangements. In these cases, trust in the rules and procedures may help sustain collaboration through times of positional churn. Accordingly, many of the examples described later in this Element rely on such rules and procedures, presenting more structured collaborative models than seen in much of the collaboration literature.

Such structures might be needed because collaborative capacity is not a universal competency in New Zealand, as reported by O'Leary (2014). The New Zealand government has several initiatives running in parallel to the Toolkit that are intended to build collaborative capacity and to select for leaders with this competency. Most notably, the New Zealand government's 'Leadership Success Profile' (State Services Commission 2017c) is used to recruit for and develop skills in nurturing public service motivation, engendering commitment to achieving goals, encouraging shared social identity, investing in relationships, and following through on procedural obligations. The team also noted distinct leadership competencies associated with each of the horizontal rows in the Toolkit, explored in Sections 3–5.

The Toolkit is focused on mechanisms for planning, decision-making, funding, and accountability. This may represent New Zealand's particular approach to NPM (Eppel and O'Leary 2021) and its obsession with accountability (Gregory 2006). However, the psychological and social aspects of collaboration are likely to be important, and given comparatively little attention in the Toolkit, even as they are taken on greater prominence in New Zealand public administration more generally.

6.2 Limitations

Determining whether this contingent model 'works' depends heavily on how we think about success in collaboration. Measuring and attributing changes in social outcomes to public policies and programmes is notoriously difficult, and attributing change to a specific collaborative approach is almost impossible (see Page 2004; Page et al. 2015). We can present no evidence that the Toolkit improved outcomes. Absent outcome measures, some authors suggest that process measures can form a useful proxy (Carey and Harris 2016). This data was not collected before the implementation of the Toolkit, so there is no point of comparison. The only data we have are the subjective reports from public servants interviewed for this Element. Without exception, they report that the Toolkit was enormously helpful in guiding decisions about collaborative arrangements. The Toolkit is still used frequently after five years. As described in Section 2, we know that ministers saw benefit in the Toolkit and took advice from public servants on how to amend legislation to fully enable all of the models. None of these facts is particularly strong evidence, and further study is required to validate the Toolkit's constructs and impact. However, the Toolkit is at least a promising proof-of-concept for contingent collaboration.

This Element relies on an insider perspective, with both authors embedded in the Public Service Commission. This has advantages, in improving access to information, but may introduce bias. We know of no research on the system design toolkit by independent researchers, and this would potentially add a useful additional perspective.

We cannot claim that the axes of the Toolkit, or the models, have been validated. The axes may or may not be the most salient dimensions on which to apply a contingent approach to collaboration, and we propose here a possible method for investigating this empirically. The models, too, require further study. They represent archetypal forms of the most successful examples of collaboration in recent New Zealand memory, but these were 'successes' only in the sense of being judged successful by practitioners. Several of the examples that served as inspiration for the models have been thoroughly evaluated elsewhere, but this is not the case for all models. Some models have in fact never been tested in the form they are described – they represent an amalgamation of features from several examples that a group of public servants judged to be suitable for combination together.

We contend that, for practitioners, the relevant comparison is not between this Toolkit and a theoretically robust contingent framework (that does not yet exist) but instead between having the Toolkit and not having one. In this regard, the perspectives offered by the interviewees were clear – the Toolkit usefully contributed to their practice and made their lives easier. Absent the Toolkit, how else might practitioners identify possible models? They could draw from their own past experiences, or those examples that they know of, in each case likely a narrower range of options than those presented in the Toolkit. And how might they choose between these? They might choose the one that they believed was most successful in addressing a prior unrelated problem context, without a structured means for considering how their current context was similar or different. Having a broad set of collaborative examples to draw from was helpful; having a means for choosing between them gave practitioners the confidence to design collaborative arrangements for solving the problems they faced.

The Toolkit has important limitations when it comes to generalizing findings for use in other contexts. The foundation of a contingent approach is the recognition that context matters. The Toolkit was applied in one jurisdiction (New Zealand), between similar actors (central government agencies). Some of the features that make this study possible – a unitary central government, a relatively small country, a history of public administration innovation and engagement with theory – are themselves reasons to believe the New Zealand experience may not be directly transferable to other countries. The Toolkit certainly represents a structured and formal approach to collaboration in a jurisdiction that is arguably overly focused on accountability (Gregory 2006). Schick (1998) famously observed that the New Zealand approach to public administration delivered significant advantages, but that most countries should not try to copy them. As elsewhere in this Element, context matters.

Governments around the world, including New Zealand, are contending with the challenge of collaborating with organizations outside of government (Osborne 2006), and this is an area where the Public Service Commission is planning future study. In particular, the Public Service Act 2020 increases the expectation on the public service to engage effectively with the indigenous Māori people, likely to be a focus of the public service for years to come. Cross-sectoral collaboration in New Zealand is the subject of another volume in this series (Eppel and O'Leary 2021). However, Eppel and O'Leary contend that New Zealand's very structured approach to collaboration, of which the Toolkit is emblematic, may act as a barrier to cross-sectoral collaboration.

We therefore conclude that the Toolkit is an interesting example of practice but not the definitive approach. Our mustering call is not that the Toolkit is the best solution, but that explicitly contingent approaches to collaboration are possible and are perceived as useful by public managers trying to collaborate.

6.3 Where to Now?

We conclude with goals for the future that set out possible pathways to developing a more robust contingency approach to collaboration. This offers suggestions for improving this Toolkit or developing others to better serve practitioners looking for guidance, and scholars looking for rigorous and validated theory.

Almost immediately upon the completion of the Toolkit, the same group that created it reflected on its solipsistic qualities – government had laboured to create a tool that enabled it to play more nicely with itself. Osborne (2006) posited that collaboration between actors both inside and outside government (rather than collaboration between agencies) is the key public administration challenge that must be solved to address our most complex problems. The development of a contingent approach to engaging with businesses, NGOs, and citizens is a current challenge for New Zealand public administration practice (O'Leary 2014), a process that in itself may require a collaborative or co-production approach (Eppel and O'Leary 2021). Although, the vast number of potential partners and their different aspirations may make it more difficult to reach agreement on a limited number of discrete models. Rhodes observed that 'if governance is constructed differently, contingently and continuously, we cannot have a tool kit for managing it' (2007, p. 1257) and called instead for a more emergent approach, where models are the 'products of diverse actions and political struggles informed by the beliefs of agents as they arise in the context of traditions' (p. 1252). Nonetheless, we intuit that practitioners would still value a contingent toolkit for cross-sectoral collaboration because this would provide at least some shared language and shared understandings on which to base the negotiation of collaborative arrangements with parties outside of government. Alternately, such a structured approach may risk 'overbureaucratisation of mandates' that impede collaborative innovation (Eppel and O'Leary 2021, p. 65).

Within the New Zealand context, the relationship between Māori and the Crown is of particular importance. New Zealand was founded in 1840 based on a treaty between the indigenous Māori and the British Crown (the Treaty of Waitangi/*te Tiriti o Waitangi*). This treaty allowed the British settlers and Māori people to live together in New Zealand. Since the signing of the treaty, it has been breached numerous times. In 1975, a tribunal was established to make recommendations on claims relating to breaches of the treaty by the Crown, as alleged by Māori, beginning a period of redress for past harms. A key challenge for the New Zealand government is to build a working relationship with Māori after this period of redress. Various documents by Māori and by the Crown call for closer working relationship and 'partnership' between the two parties (Charters et al. 2019; Davis 2019), and the Public Service Act 2020 requires the public service to improve its ability to engage with Māori. Engagement with Māori takes many forms and may be well suited to a contingent approach for designing different arrangements. We understand that this is under current consideration between Māori and government agencies.

These possible extensions of the toolkit represent a deepening of the application of contingent collaboration in the practice of New Zealand public servants. This would take contingent collaboration beyond an interagency context, and into the cross-sectoral context described by Ansell and Gash (2008) and Bryson et al. (2015).

Additionally, the contingent model could expand laterally, into other jurisdictions. A similar method could be employed in order to develop a Toolkit that worked in another context – a group of practitioners with broad experience in the different forms of collaboration attempted in that jurisdiction could be brought together to carefully reflect on past experiences, collect cases, and inductively observe how and why these cases group or differentiate. Some differences could be expected from the New Zealand model, for example: relating to State and Provincial governments in Australia, the United States, and Canada; or devolution and the strengthened role of local governments in the United Kingdom and much of Europe. Nonetheless, observing how the dimensions of a contingent framework in another jurisdiction were similar or different to that in New Zealand, would give some indication of the extent to which New Zealand's Toolkit describes generalizable phenomena.

Our final proposal for advancing contingent approaches to collaboration is to seek to bring theory and practice more closely together. Public administration literature is filled with examples of case studies of collaborative arrangements. An earlier paper (Lee and Scott 2019) proposed a meta-analysis of past collaboration literature, using a qualitative comparative analysis methodology (Schneider and Wagemann 2012) to group case studies based on similarities and differences in their problem contexts, and mapping these against findings reported in the studies to determine predictive and associative factors for collaborative success. Thus, the Toolkit could be validated (or refuted) based on the sum of existing literature, and a more generalizable contingent framework could be created. A further consideration is the evolution of contingencies over time – several examples described in this Element involved collaborative approaches shifting from one model to another over several years; a possible extension would be to look at contextual factors or success markers in shifting between models, building on the idea of 'collaborative evolution' as described by Ulibarri et al. (2020).

This Element aims to provide examples and ideas for practitioners, while also providing a starting point for a further research approach. Interagency collaboration is still the holy grail and philosopher's stone of public administration practice, and scholarship must find a way to help practitioners to design effective collaborative methods. More specifically, practitioners are clamouring for an answer to the question of when to use which collaborative models.

Appendix 1: Data Sources

This Element combines data from several sources:

- participant–observer field notes from during the formation of the Toolkit;
- document analysis of the Toolkit and surrounding documents;
- internal and external evaluations of different models described in the Element;
- a literature review of collaboration, interagency collaboration, and contingency;
- interviews with the original project team that developed the Toolkit; and
- interviews with leaders from each of the embedded element examples.

Previously published evaluations include Scott and Boyd 2016, 2017, 2020, 2022; Corbett et al. 2018 2020; Scott and Bardach 2019; Scott and Merton 2020; Hughes and Scott 2021.

The Element draws from ninety-four interviews with New Zealand public service leaders. Quotes are drawn from semi-structured interviews conducted for the purpose of the Element, except for:

- Andrew Coster, Audrey Sonerson, Aphra Green, Paul O'Connell, and Oliver Valins, who were interviewed by the authors for the purpose of case study material in the Australia and New Zealand School of Government library (see Scott 2017);
- Erin Judge, Kevin Allan, Phil Griffiths, Jeff Montgomery, Karen Guilliland, and Lois van Waardenberg, interviewed as part of separate case studies on behalf of the Public Service Commission; and
- an independent evaluation of place-based initiatives (Litmus 2019).

Appendix 2: Further Reading

The Toolkit and associated guidance are available on the Public Service Commission website at:
www.publicservice.govt.nz/resources/mog-shared-problems/
Further reading on each of the case studies can be found here:Natural Resources Sector
www.beehive.govt.nz/sites/default/files/2017-12/Natural%20Resources.pdf
Justice Sector Leadership Board
https://justice.govt.nz/justice-sector-policy/about-the-justice-sector/
Border Executive Board
www.customs.govt.nz/about-us/border-executive-board/
Social Wellbeing Agency
https://swa.govt.nz/
Government Economics Network
www.gen.org.nz
Government Legal Network
www.gln.govt.nz/; https://www.publicservice.govt.nz/resources/bps-spotlight-gln/
Government Chief Digital Officer
www.digital.govt.nz/
The Treasury
www.treasury.govt.nz
Procurement Functional Lead
www.procurement.govt.nz/about-us/functional-leadership/
Auckland Policy Office
www.govt.nz/organisations/auckland-policy-office/
Children's Teams
https://thehub.swa.govt.nz/assets/documents/Childrens-Teams-Assessment_0.pdf
South Auckland Social Wellbeing Board
https://saswb.com/
SmartStart
https://smartstart.services.govt.nz/ www.publicservice.govt.nz/resources/bps-result10-cs3/

Glossary

Agency – A general term for a public organization, including departments, ministries, commissions, and arms-length bodies. In New Zealand, 'departments' refers to agencies that are part of the legal Crown, and 'agencies' refers to both departments <u>and</u> public organizations that are separate legal entities.

Auckland Policy Office/APO – A shared office space in Auckland that co-locates employees from seventeen government agencies.

Cabinet – The New Zealand Government's body of senior ministers, broadly following the traditions of the UK cabinet system. Cabinet is not established by statute but instead exists by convention. Cabinet forms part of the executive branch of government, and formulates government policy. Not all ministers are members of Cabinet. Members are bound by cabinet collective responsibility, which requires that members publicly approve of its collective decisions or else resign.

Chief Executive – The administrative head of an agency, known elsewhere as 'Secretary', 'Permanent Secretary', 'Direct-General', or 'Deputy Minister'/'*sous-ministre*'. New Zealand chief executives operate under a more delegated public service bargain than in many other jurisdictions. The Cabinet manual discourages ministers from interfering in the operation of agencies, which means that chief executives have greater autonomy and responsibility than international equivalents.

Contingent approach/contingency – The discretionary application of management solutions to meet specific contexts, first described in the 1950s and 1960s in response to a dissatisfaction with universal approaches.

Dimensional framework – The mapping of problem contexts to solutions along two or more categorical axes following an if/then operational logic.

Government Chief Digital Office/GCDO – A designated position within the New Zealand public service with overall responsibility for information and communication technology.

Government Economic Network/GEN – A professional network for economists and those interested in using economics in the New Zealand public service.

Government Legal Network/GLN – A professional network for lawyers in the New Zealand public service.

Information and communication technology/ICT – Any technological product that stores, manipulates, transmits, or receives information electronically.

Interagency collaboration – An inclusive term used to describe a range of practices that involve government agencies working together to solve shared problems. Inclusive of cooperation, coordination, and collaboration. Overlaps with 'horizontal management' and 'joined-up government'.

Layer – One of the three horizontal rows of the 'Toolkit for Shared Problems', referring to problems of public policy, public administration, or service delivery.

Minister of the Crown/Minister – A member of Parliament who also holds a ministerial warrant from the Crown to perform specified functions of government. Ministers are appointed by the governor-general following advice of the prime minister. Each agency has a responsible minister, but agencies may also support more than one minister, and each minister may be responsible for more than one agency.

Model – One of eighteen archetypal forms for interagency collaboration described in the Toolkit for Shared Problems. These may be based on past examples or combine elements from multiple examples.

New Public Management/NPM – A loose collection of administrative reforms popularized in the 1980s and 1990s, characterized by autonomy for public servants associated with accountability for what they achieved. Influenced by agency and public choice theories. New Zealand was generally considered the purest example of NPM reforms.

Non-government organization/NGO – A nonprofit entity independent of government, also known as civil society organization, nonprofit organization, or not-for-profit organization.

Public servant/public administrator/practitioner – Used interchangeably to refer to members of New Zealand's permanent politically neutral civil service.

Public Service Commission/er – 'State Services Commission/er' until 2020. The Public Service Commissioner is the head of the New Zealand public service, responsible for (among other things) advising the government on structures and governance arrangements, appointing and managing chief executives, and managing the integrity and behaviour of the public service. The Commission is an agency established to support the Commissioner with performing their duties and functions.

Toolkit for Shared Problems/The Toolkit – A guidance document issued by the Public Service Commission that proposes certain administrative and governance arrangements as being more suitable for responding to certain problem contexts. Based on a contingent, dimensional framework and consisting of eighteen 'models'.

References

Agranoff, R. (1991). Human services integration: Past and present challenges in public administration. *Public Administration Review*, *51*(6), 533–42.

Agranoff, R. (2004). *Collaborative public management: New strategies for local governments*. Georgetown University Press.

Agranoff, R. (2017). *Crossing boundaries for intergovernmental management*. Georgetown University Press.

Agranoff, R., & McGuire, M. (2003). Inside the matrix: Integrating the paradigms of intergovernmental and network management. *International Journal of Public Administration*, *26*(12), 1401–22.

Alford, J. (2002). Why do public-sector clients coproduce? Toward a contingency theory. *Administration & Society*, *34*(1), 32–56.

Ansell, C., & Gash, A. (2008). Collaborative governance in theory and practice. *Journal of Public Administration Research and Theory*, *18*(4), 543–71.

Axelsson, R., & Axelsson, S. B. (2006). Integration and collaboration in public health – a conceptual framework. *The International Journal of Health Planning and Management*, *21*(1), 75–88.

Baehler, K. (2003). 'Managing for outcomes': Accountability and thrust. *Australian Journal of Public Administration*, *62*(4), 23–34.

Bardach, E. (1998). *Getting agencies to work together: The practice and theory of managerial craftsmanship*. Brookings Institution Press.

Bardach, E. (2001). Developmental dynamics: Interagency collaboration as an emergent phenomenon. *Journal of Public Administration Research and Theory*, *11*(2), 149–64.

Bevir, M. (2012). *Governance: A very short introduction*. Oxford University Press.

Bingham, L. B., & O'Leary, R. (2006). Conclusion: Parallel play, not collaboration: Missing questions, missing connections. *Public Administration Review*, *66*(Suppl. 1), 161–167.

Blake, R. R., & Mouton, J. S. (1964). *The managerial grid.: The key to leadership excellence*. Gulf.

Bogdanor, V. (Ed.). (2005). *Joined-up government*. Oxford University Press.

Bommert, B. (2010). Collaborative innovation in the public sector. *International Public Management Review*, *11*(1), 15–33.

Boston, J., Martin, J., Pallot, J., & Walsh, P. (1996). *Public management: The New Zealand model*. Oxford University Press.

Bowman, A. O. M., & Parsons, B. M. (2013). Making connections: Performance regimes and extreme events. *Public Administration Review*, *73*(1), 63–73.

Brewer, M. B., & Hewstone, M. E. (2004). *Self and social identity.* Blackwell.

Brown, K., & Keast, R. (2003). Citizen-government engagement: Community connection through networked arrangements. *Asian Journal of Public Administration, 25*(1), 107–31.

Bryson, J. M., Crosby, B. C., & Stone, M. (2015). Designing and Implementing Cross-Sector Collaborations: Needed *and* Challenging. *Public Administration Review, 75*(5), 647–63.

Carey, G., & Crammond, B. (2015). What works in joined-up government? An evidence synthesis. *International Journal of Public Administration, 38* (13–14), 1020–29.

Carey, G., & Harris, P. (2016). Developing management practices to support joined-up governance. *Australian Journal of Public Administration, 75*(1), 112–18.

Charters, C., Kingdon-Bebb, K., Olsen, T. et al. (2019). *He Puapua: Report of the working group on a plan to realise the UN declaration on the rights of indigenous peoples in Aotearoa/New Zealand.* Technical working group on a plan to realise the UN declaration on the rights of indigenous peoples in Aotearoa/New Zealand, Auckland.

Chen, B. (2010). Antecedents or processes? Determinants of perceived effectiveness of interorganizational collaborations for public service delivery. *International Public Management Journal, 13*(4), 381–407.

Christensen, M., & Yoshimi, H. (2003). Public sector performance reporting: New public management and contingency theory insights. *Government Auditing Review, 10*(3), 71–83.

Corbett, J., Grube, D. C., Lovell, H., & Scott, R. J. (2018). Singular memory or institutional memories? Toward a dynamic approach. *Governance, 31*(3), 555–73.

Corbett, J., Grube, D. C., Lovell, H., & Scott, R. J. (2020). *Institutional memory as storytelling.* Cambridge University Press.

Cordes, C. (2015). *Our Customer Research.* Department of Internal Affairs, Wellington. https://www.digital.govt.nz/blog/our-customer-research/

Craft, J., & Halligan, J. (2020). *Advising governments in the Westminster tradition: Policy advisory systems in Australia, Britain, Canada and New Zealand.* Cambridge University Press.

Cristofoli, D., Trivellato, B., & Verzillo, S. (2019). Network management as a contingent activity: A configurational analysis of managerial behaviors in different network settings. *Public Management Review, 21*(12), 1775–800.

Darlington, Y., Feeney, J. A., & Rixon, K. (2005). Interagency collaboration between child protection and mental health services: Practices, attitudes and barriers. *Child Abuse & Neglect, 29*(10), 1085–98.

Davies, J. S. (2002). The governance of urban regeneration: A critique of the 'governing without government' thesis. *Public Administration, 80*(2), 301–22.

Davies, J. S. (2009). The limits of joined-up government: Towards a political analysis. *Public Administration, 87*(1), 80–96.

Davies, J. S. (2012). Network governance theory: A Gramscian critique. *Environment and Planning A, 44*(11), 2687–704.

Davis, K. (2019). *Building closer partnerships with Māori: Proactive release of Cabinet paper and MCR-19-MIN-0004.* New Zealand Government, Wellington.

Dawkins, R. (1981). In defence of selfish genes. *Philosophy, 56*(218), 556–73.

Diaz-Kope, L., Miller-Stevens, K., & Morris, J. C. (2015). Collaboration processes and institutional structure: Reexamining the black box. *International Journal of Public Administration, 38*(9), 607–15.

Diaz-Kope, L. M., & Morris, J. C. (2019). *Organizational motivation for collaboration: Theory and evidence.* Rowman & Littlefield.

Doberstein, C. (2016). Designing collaborative governance decision-making in search of a 'collaborative advantage'. *Public Management Review, 18*(6), 819–41.

Donadelli, F., & Lodge, M. (2019). Machinery of Government Reforms in New Zealand. *Policy Quarterly, 15*(4), 43–48.

Donahue, J. (2004). *On collaborative governance.* Corporate social responsibility initiative working paper 2. Kennedy School of Government, Harvard University.

Douglas, M. (1982). *Introduction to grid/group analysis.* Routledge.

Dunleavy, P., & Hood, C. (1994). From old public administration to new public management. *Public Money & Management, 14*(3), 9–16.

Elston, T., & Dixon, R. (2020). The effect of shared service centers on administrative intensity in English local government: A longitudinal evaluation. *Journal of Public Administration Research and Theory, 30*(1), 113–29.

Emerson, K., & Nabatchi, T. (2015). *Collaborative governance regimes.* Georgetown University Press.

Emerson, K., Nabatchi, T., & Balogh, S. (2012). An integrative framework for collaborative governance. *Journal of Public Administration Research & Theory, 22*(1), 1–29.

Eppel, E., Gill, D., Lips, M., & Ryan, B. (2013). The cross-organizational collaboration solution? Conditions, roles and dynamics in New Zealand. In: O'Flynn, J., Blackman, D., & Halligan, J. (Eds.), *Crossing Boundaries in Public Management and Policy* (pp. 67–83). Routledge.

Eppel, E., & O'Leary, R. (2021). *Retrofitting collaboration into the new public management: Evidence from New Zealand.* Cambridge University Press.

Fiedler, F. E. (1964). A contingency model of leadership effectiveness. In: Berkowitz, L. (Ed)., *Advances in experimental social psychology* (Vol. 1, pp. 149–90). Academic Press.

Fiedler, F. E. (1993). The contingency model: New directions for leadership utilization. In: Matteson, M. T. & Ivancevich, J. M. (Eds.), *Management and Organizational Behavior Classics* (pp. 333–45). Richard D Irwin.

Gajda, R. (2004). Utilizing collaboration theory to evaluate strategic alliances. *American Journal of Evaluation, 25*(1), 65–77.

Getha-Taylor, H. (2019). *Partnerships that last: Identifying the keys to resilient collaboration.* Cambridge University Press.

Getha-Taylor, H., Grayer, M. J., Kempf, R. J., & O'Leary, R. (2019). Collaborating in the absence of trust? What collaborative governance theory and practice can learn from the literatures of conflict resolution, psychology, and law. *The American Review of Public Administration, 49*(1), 51–64.

Government Legal Network (GLN). (2014). *About the network.* www.gln.govt.nz/about-the-network/

Gray, B. (1989). *Collaborating: Finding common ground for multiparty problems.* Jossey-Bass.

Greenwood, R., Hinings, C. R., & Ranson, S. (1975). Contingency theory and the organization of local authorities. Part I: Differentiation and integration. *Public Administration, 53*(1), 1–23.

Gregory, R. (2006). Theoretical faith and practical works: De-autonomizing and joining-up in the New Zealand state sector. In: Christensen, T. and Lægrid, P. (Eds.), *Autonomy and Regulation: Coping with Agencies in the Modern State* (pp. 137–61). Edward Elgar Publishing.

Gregson, B. A., Cartlidge, A. M., & Bond, J. (1992). Development of a measure of professional collaboration in primary health care. *Journal of Epidemiology & Community Health, 46*(1), 48–53.

Hagebak, B. R. (1979). Local human service delivery: The integration imperative. *Public Administration Review, 39*(6), 575–82.

Halligan, J. (2004). *Civil service systems in Anglo-American countries.* Edward Elgar.

Hanleybrown, F., Kania, J., & Kramer, M. (2012). *Channeling change: Making collective impact work* (pp. 56–78). FSG.

Hattori, R. A., & Lapidus, T. (2004). Collaboration, trust and innovative change. *Journal of Change Management, 4*(2), 97–104.

Hayes, S. C., Wilson, K. G., Gifford, E. V., Follette, V. M., & Strosahl, K. (1996). Experiential avoidance and behavioral disorders: A functional dimensional approach to diagnosis and treatment. *Journal of Consulting and Clinical Psychology, 64*(6), 1152.

Head, B. W. (2013). The collaboration solution? Factors for collaborative success. In: O'Flynn, J., Blackman, D., & Halligan, J. (Eds.), *Crossing Boundaries in Public Management and Policy* (pp. 162–77). Routledge.

Hersey, P., & Blanchard, K. (1969). *Management of organizational behavior: Utilizing human resources* (p. 84). Prentice Hall.

Hinings, C. R., Greenwood, R., & Ranson, S. (1975). Contingency theory and the organization of local authorities: Part II contingencies and structure. *Public Administration, 53*(2), 169–94.

Hipkins, C. (2019a). *Organisations of the public service.* Cabinet Paper CPC-19-SUB-0011. New Zealand Government, Wellington.

Hipkins, C. (2019b). *A unified public service.* Cabinet Paper CPC-19-SUB-0007. New Zealand Government, Wellington.Hipkins, C. (2019c). Announcement of Public Service Reforms, Speech delivered at Victoria University of Wellington, Wellington, on 26 June 2019. www.beehive.govt.nz/speech/announcement-public-service-reforms

Hood, C. (2000). Paradoxes of public-sector managerialism, old public management and public service bargains. *International Public Management Journal, 3*(1), 1–22.

Horwath, J., & Morrison, T. (2007). Collaboration, integration and change in children's services: Critical issues and key ingredients. *Child Abuse & Neglect, 31*(1), 55–69.

Hovik, S., & Hanssen, G. S. (2015). The impact of network management and complexity on multi-level coordination. *Public Administration, 93*, 506–23.

Hughes, P. & Scott, R. J. (2021). High-autonomy and High-alignment: Coordinating a more unified public service. In: Richardson J. & Mazey S. (Eds.) Policy-making Under Pressure: Rethinking the policy process in Aotearoa New Zealand. Canterbury University Press. 170–179.

Huxham, C., & Macdonald, D. (1992). Introducing collaborative advantage: Achieving interorganizational effectiveness through meta-strategy. *Management Decision, 30*(3), 50–6.

Huxham, C., & Vangen, S. (2000). Leadership in the shaping and implementation of collaboration agendas: How things happen in a (not quite) joined-up world. *Academy of Management Journal, 43*(6), 1159–75.

Huxham, C., & Vangen, S. (2013). *Managing to collaborate: The theory and practice of collaborative advantage.* Routledge.

Imperial, M. T. (2005). Using collaboration as a governance strategy: Lessons from six watershed management programs. *Administration & Society, 37*(3), 281–320.

Ingham, A. G., Levinger, G., Graves, J., & Peckham, V. (1974). The Ringelmann effect: Studies of group size and group performance. *Journal of Experimental Social Psychology, 10*(4), 371–84.

Ingram, J. K. (1888). *A history of political economy.* The Macmillan Company. (Reprint, Augustus M. Kelley, 1967.)

Blavatnik School of Government. (2019). *International Civil Service Effectiveness Index.*

Jennings Jr, E. T., & Krane, D. (1994). Coordination and welfare reform: The quest for the philosopher's stone. *Public Administration Review, 54*(4), 341–8.

Jensen, K., Scott, R. J., Slocombe, L., Boyd, R., & Cowey, L. (2014). *The management and organisational challenges of more joined-up government: New Zealand's Better Public Services reforms.* New Zealand Government, Wellington.

Jones, C., Hesterly, W. S., & Borgatti, S. P. (1997). A general theory of network governance: Exchange conditions and social mechanisms. *Academy of Management Review, 22*(4), 911–45.

Juillet, L., & Rasmussen, K. (2008). *Defending a contested ideal: Merit and the public service commission, 1908–2008* (p. 264). University of Ottawa Press/ Les Presses de l'Université d'Ottawa.

Kania, J., & Kramer, M. (2011). *Collective impact.* FSG.

Keast, R., Brown, K., & Mandell, M. (2007). Getting the right mix: Unpacking integration meanings and strategies. *International Public Management Journal, 10*(1), 9–33.

Keast, R., Mandell, M., & Brown, K. (2006). Mixing state, market and network governance modes: The role of government in 'crowded' policy domains. *International Journal of Organization Theory & Behavior, 9*(1), 27–50.

Kettl, D. F., & Kelman, S. (2007). *Reflections on 21st century government management.* IBM Business of Government.

Koppenjan, J. F. M., & Klijn, E. H. (2004). *Managing uncertainties in networks: A network approach to problem solving and decision making.* Psychology Press.

Krueger, E. L. (2005). *A transaction costs explanation of inter-local government collaboration.* University of North Texas.

Kurtz, C. F., & Snowden, D. J. (2003). The new dynamics of strategy: Sense-making in a complex and complicated world. *IBM Systems Journal, 42*(3), 462–83.

Kwon, S. W., & Feiock, R. C. (2010). Overcoming the barriers to cooperation: Intergovernmental service agreements. *Public Administration Review, 70*(6), 876–84.

Laan, A., Noorderhaven, N., Voordijk, H., & Dewulf, G. (2011). Building trust in construction partnering projects: An exploratory case-study. *Journal of Purchasing and Supply Management, 17*(2), 98–108.

State Services Commission. (2017)c. *Leadership Success Profile.* Wellington.

Lee, E., Esaki, N., & Greene, R. (2009). Collocation: Integrating child welfare and substance abuse services. *Journal of Social Work Practice in the Addictions, 9*(1), 55–70.

Lee, M., & Scott, R. J. (2019). A contingency theory of collaboration: When to use which methods? In: *International Research Society for Public Management Conference*, Wellington.

Litmus. (2019). *Implementation and emerging outcomes evaluation of the Place-Based Initiatives.*

Locke, E. A., Latham, G. P., & Erez, M. (1988). The determinants of goal commitment. *Academy of Management Review, 13*(1), 23–39.

Lodge, M., & Gill, D. (2011). Toward a new era of administrative reform? The myth of post-NPM in New Zealand. *Governance, 24*(1), 141–66.

Lonti, Z., & Gregory, R. (2007). Accountability or countability? Performance measurement in the New Zealand public service, 1992–2002. *Australian Journal of Public Administration, 66*(4), 468–84.

State Services Commission. (2018). *Machinery of government: Toolkit for Shared Problems.* Wellington.

Mansbridge, J. (2014). A contingency theory of accountability. In: Bovens, M., Goodin, R. E., & Schillemans, T. (Eds.), *The Oxford Handbook of Public Accountability.* Oxford University Press. 55–68.

March, J. G., & Simon, H. A. (1958). *Organizations.* Wiley.

Marrett, C. (1971). On the specification of interorganizational dimensions. *Sociology and Social Research, 56*(1), 83–9.

Marsh, D., & McConnell, A. (2010). Towards a framework for establishing policy success. *Public Administration, 88*(2), 564–83.

McGrandle, J. (2017). Understanding diversity management in the public sector: A case for contingency theory. *International Journal of Public Administration, 40*(6), 526–37.

McGuire, M. (2002). Managing networks: Propositions on what managers do and why they do it. *Public Administration Review, 62*(5), 599–601.

McGuire, M. (2006). Collaborative public management: Assessing what we know and how we know it. *Public Administration Review, 66*(1), 33–43.

Memon, A. R., & Kinder, T. (2017). Co-location as a catalyst for service innovation: A study of Scottish health and social care. *Public Management Review, 19*(4), 381–405.

Ministry of Justice. (2021). *About the justice sector: The justice sector leadership board*. www.justice.govt.nz/justice-sector-policy/about-the-justice-sector /#board

Noonan, P. M., Morningstar, M. E., & Gaumer-Erickson, A. (2008). Improving interagency collaboration: Effective strategies used by high-performing local districts and communities. *Career Development for Exceptional Individuals, 31*(3), 132–43.

Norman, R., & Gill, D. (2011). Restructuring: An over-used lever for change in New Zealand's state sector? In: Ryan, B., & Gill, D. (Eds.), *Future State: Directions for Public Management in New Zealand* (pp. 262–80). Victoria University Press.

O'Flynn, J. (2013a). Crossing boundaries in public management and policy: An introduction. In: O'Flynn, J., Blackman, D., & Halligan, J. (Eds.), *Crossing Boundaries in Public Management and Policy* (pp. 3–10). Routledge.

O'Flynn, J., Blackman, D., & Halligan, J. (Eds.). (2013). *Crossing Boundaries in Public Management and Policy*. Routledge.

O'Flynn, J., Buick, F., Blackman, D., & Halligan, J. (2011). You win some, you lose some: Experiments with joined-up government. *International Journal of Public Administration, 34*(4), 244–54.

O'Leary, R. (2014). *Collaborative governance in New Zealand: Important choices ahead*. Fulbright New Zealand.

O'Leary, R., & Vij, N. (2012). Collaborative public management: Where have we been and where are we going? *The American Review of Public Administration, 42*(5), 507–22.

O'Toole, L. J., & Meier, K. (2004). Public management in intergovernmental networks: Matching structural and behavioral networks. *Journal of Public Administration Research & Theory, 14*(4), 469–94.

Oliver, A. (2019). *Reciprocity and the art of behavioural public policy*. Cambridge University Press.

Organisation for Economic Cooperation and Development (OECD). (2021). *Government at a Glance*. OECD Publishing. https://doi.org/10.1787/1c258 f55-en.

Osborne, D., & Gaebler, T. (1992). *Reinventing government: How the entrepreneurial spirit is transforming the public sector*. Addison.

Osborne, S. P. (2006). *The new public governance?* Taylor and Francis.

Ostrom, E. (1998). A behavioral approach to the rational choice theory of collective action. *American Political Science Review, 92*(1), 1–22.

Ouchi, W. G. (1979). A conceptual framework for the design of organizational control mechanisms. *Management Science, 25*(9), 833–48.

Page, S. (2004). Measuring accountability for results in interagency collaboratives. *Public Administration Review, 64*(5), 591–606.

Page, S. B., Stone, M. M., Bryson, J. M., & Crosby, B. C. (2015). Public value creation by cross-sector collaborations: A framework and challenges of assessment. *Public Administration, 93*(3), 715–32.

Pallott, J. (1999). Beyond NPM: Developing strategic capacity. *Financial Accountability & Management, 15*(3–4), 419–26.

Perry, J. L. (1996). Measuring public service motivation: An assessment of construct reliability and validity. *Journal of Public Administration Research and Theory, 6*(1), 5–22.

Perry, J. L. (1997). Antecedents of public service motivation. *Journal of Public Administration Research and Theory, 7*(2), 181–97.

Perry, J. L., & Hondeghem, A. (2008). Building theory and empirical evidence about public service motivation. *International Public Management Journal, 11*(1), 3–12.

Peters, B. G. (2015). *Pursuing horizontal management: The politics of public sector coordination.* University Press of Kansas.

Peters, B. G. (1998). Managing Horizontal Government: The Politics of Co-Ordination. *Public Administration, 76*(2), 295–311.

Peters, B. G., & Pierre, J. (1998). Governance without government? Rethinking public administration. *Journal of Public Administration Research and Theory, 8*(2), 223–43.

Pollitt, C., & Bouckaert, G. (2011). *Continuity and change in public policy and management.* Edward Elgar.

Prentice, C. R., Imperial, M. T., & Brudney, J. L. (2019). Conceptualizing the collaborative toolbox: A dimensional approach to collaboration. *The American Review of Public Administration, 49*(7), 792–809.

Provan, K., & Kenis, P. (2008). Modes of network governance: Structure, management, and effectiveness. *Journal of Public Administration Research and Theory, 18*(2), 229–52.

Provan, K. G., & Milward, H. B. (2001). Do networks really work? A framework for evaluating public-sector organizational networks. *Public Administration Review, 61*(4), 414–23.

Public Service Act 2020. Parliament of New Zealand.

State Services Commission. (2017a). *Better public services result 10 – SmartStart makes it easy for parents.* New Zealand Government. www.publicservice.govt.nz/resources/bps-result10-cs3/

State Services Commission. (2017b). *Government legal network: A pathway for shared success.* New Zealand Government. www.publicservice.govt.nz/resources/bps-spotlight-gln/

Ren, W., Beard, R. W., & Atkins, E. M. (2005, June). A survey of consensus problems in multi-agent coordination. In: *Proceedings of the 2005, American Control Conference* (pp. 1859–64), IEEE.

State Serives Commission. (2011). *Report of the Better Public Services Advisory Group*. New Zealand. www.publicservice.govt.nz/assets/Legacy/resources/bps-report-nov2011_0.pdf

Rhodes, R. A. W. (2007). Understanding governance: Ten years on. *Organization Studies, 28*(8), 1243–64.

Sadoff, C. W., & Grey, D. (2005). Cooperation on international rivers: A continuum for securing and sharing benefits. *Water International, 30*(4), 420–7.

Schick, A. (1998). Why most developing countries should not try New Zealand's reforms. *The World Bank Research Observer, 13*(1), 123–31.

Schick, A. (2001). *Reflections on the New Zealand model*. State Services Commission, Wellington.

Schmidt, W. H., & Tannenbaum, R. (1960). Management of differences. *Harvard Business Review, 38*(6), 107–115.

Schneider, C. Q., & Wagemann, C. (2012). *Set-theoretic methods for the social sciences: A guide to qualitative comparative analysis*. Cambridge University Press.

Scott, G. C. (2001). *Public sector management in New Zealand: Lessons and challenges*. Australian National University Press.

Scott, R. J. (2017). *Interagency collaboration to reduce crime in New Zealand*. Australia and New Zealand School of Government.

Scott, R. J. (2019). Public service motivation and social identity. In: *International Research Society for Public Management Conference*, Wellington.

Scott, R. J., & Bardach, E. (2019). A comparison of management adaptations for joined-up government: Lessons from New Zealand. *Australian Journal of Public Administration, 78*(2), 191–212.

Scott, R. J., & Boyd, R. (2016). Results, targets and measures to drive collaboration: Lessons from the New Zealand Better Public Services reforms. In: Butcher, J., & Gilchrist, D. (Eds.), *The Three Sector Solution: Delivering public policy in collaboration with not-for-profits and business* (pp. 235–57). Australian National University Press.

Scott, R. J., & Boyd, R. (2017). Joined-up for what? Response to Carey and Harris on adaptive collaboration. *Australian Journal of Public Administration, 76*(1), 138–44.

Scott, R. J., & Boyd, R. (2020). Determined to succeed: Can goal commitment sustain interagency collaboration? *Public Policy and Administration* (April). http://doi.org/10.1177/0952076720905002

Scott, R. J., & Boyd, R. (2022). *Targeting commitment: Interagency perform-ance in New Zealand*. Brookings Institution Press.

Scott, R. J., Donadelli, F., Merton, E. R. K. (Forthcoming). *Administrative Philosophies in the Discourse and Decisions of the New Zealand Public Service: Is post-NPM still a myth?* International Review of Administrative Sciences.

Scott, R. J., & Macaulay, M. (2020). Making sense of New Zealand's 'spirit of service': Social identity and the civil service. *Public Money & Management, 40*(8), 579–88.

Scott, R. J., Macaulay, M., & Merton, E. K. (2020, 5–6 December). Drawing new boundaries: Can we legislate for administrative behaviour? In: *Public Administration Review Symposium – Decision-Making in Public Organisations: The Continued Relevance of Administrative Behaviour*, London.

Scott, R. J., & Merton, E. R. K. (2021). When the going gets tough, the goal-committed get going: Overcoming the transaction costs of inter-agency collaborative governance. *Public Management Review, 23*(11), 1640–1663..

Sedgwick, D. (2017). Building collaboration: Examining the relationship between collaborative processes and activities. *Journal of Public Administration Research and Theory, 27*(2), 236–52.

Shelton, L. (2013). *Al Morrison Leaving Conservation Dept, joining State Services Commission*. Wellington Scoop. http://wellington.scoop.co.nz/?p=54803

Sørensen, E., & Torfing, J. (2016). *Theories of democratic network governance*. Springer.

State Services Commission (2001) *Report of the Advisory Group on the Review of the Centre. New Zealand Government*, Wellington. https://www.publicservice.govt.nz/assets/Legacy/resources/review_of_centre.pdf

Sullivan, H., & Skelcher, C. (2017). *Working across boundaries: Collaboration in public services*. Macmillan International Higher Education.

Sullivan, H., Williams, P., & Jeffares, S. (2012). Leadership for collaboration: Situated agency in practice. *Public Management Review, 14*(1), 41–66.

Susskind, L., McKearnan, S., & Thomas-Larmer, J. (1999). *The consensus-building handbook: A comprehensive guide to reaching agreement*. Sage.

Tajfel, H. (1974). Social identity and intergroup behaviour. *Social Science Information, 13*(2), 65–93.

Talbot, C., & Talbot, C. (2013). The structure solution? Public sector mergers in the United Kingdom. In: O'Flynn, J., Blackman, D., & Halligan, J. (Eds.), *Crossing Boundaries in Public Management and Policy* (pp. 67–83). Routledge.

Takahashi, L. M., & Smutny, G. (2002). Collaborative windows and organizational governance: Exploring the formation and demise of social service partnerships. *Nonprofit and Voluntary Sector Quarterly, 31*(2), 165–85.

Tannenbaum, R., & Schmidt, H. S. (1957). How to choose a leadership pattern. *Harvard Business Review*, March-April, 95–101.

Taylor, F. W. (2004). *Scientific management*. Routledge.

Thompson, D. F. (2014). Responsibility for failures of government: The problem of many hands. *The American Review of Public Administration, 44*(3), 259–73.

Thomson, A. M. (2001). *Collaboration: Meaning and measurement*. Indiana University.

Thomson, A. M., & Perry, J. L. (1998). Can AmeriCorps build communities? *Nonprofit and Voluntary Sector Quarterly, 27*(4), 399–420.

Thomson, A. M., & Perry, J. L. (2006). Collaboration processes: Inside the black box. *Public Administration Review, 66*(1), 20–32.

Thornton, D. (2018). *Professionalising Whitehall: Responsibilities of the Head of Function for Digital, Data and Technology*. Institute for Government. www.instituteforgovernment.org.uk/publications/professionalisingwhite hall-responsibilities-head-function-digital-data-and-technology

The Treasury (2006) *Review of Central Agencies' Role in Promoting and Assuring State Sector Performance*. New Zealand Government, Wellington. https://www.treasury.govt.nz/sites/default/files/2007-11/tsy-exgrev-ca-sep06.pdf

The Treasury. (2021). *Internal controls*. www.treasury.govt.nz/information-and-services/state-sector-leadership/guidance/internal-controls

Tschannen-Moran, M. (2001). Collaboration and the need for trust. *Journal of Educational Administration, 39*(4), 308–31.

Ulibarri, N., Emerson, K., Imperial, M. T. et al. (2020). How does collaborative governance evolve? Insights from a medium-n case comparison. *Policy and Society, 39*(4), 617–37.

Van Huyck, J. B., Battalio, R. C., & Beil, R. O. (1990). Tacit coordination games, strategic uncertainty, and coordination failure. *The American Economic Review, 80*(1), 234–48.

Vangen, S., & Huxham, C. (2003). Nurturing collaborative relations: Building trust in interorganizational collaboration. *The Journal of Applied Behavioral Science, 39*(1), 5–31.

Vitalis, H., & Scott, R. J. (2015). Joint ventures in the public sector: Translating lessons from the private sector to New Zealand government departments. In: *Australia and New Zealand Academy of Management Conference*, Queenstown.

Verhoest, K., & Bouckaert, G. (2005). Machinery of government and policy capacity: The effects of specialization and coordination. In: Painter, M., & Pierre, J. (Eds.), *Challenges to State Policy Capacity* (pp. 92–111). Palgrave Macmillan.

Verweij, S., Klijn, E. H., Edelenbos, J., & Van Buuren, M. W. (2013). What makes governance networks work? A fuzzy set qualitative comparative analysis of 14 Dutch spatial planning projects. *Public Administration, 91*(4), 1035–55.

Waardenburg, M., Groenleer, M., deJong, J., & Keijser, B. (2020). Paradoxes of collaborative governance: Investigating the real-life dynamics of multi-agency collaborations using a quasi-experimental action-research approach. *Public Management Review, 22*(3), 386–407.

Walter, U. M., & Petr, C. G. (2000). A template for family-centred interagency collaboration. *Families in Society, 81*(5), 494–503.

Weber, C., Haugh, H., Göbel, M., & Leonardy, H. (2021). Pathways to lasting cross-sector social collaboration: A configurational study. *Journal of Business Ethics*, 1–27. https://doi.org/10.1007/s10551-020-04714-y

Williamson, O. E. (1979). Transaction-cost economics: The governance of contractual relations. *The Journal of Law and Economics, 22*(2), 233–61.

Wilson, J. Q. (Ed.). (1989). *Bureaucracy: What government agencies do and why they do it*. Basic Books.

Woodward, J. (1965). *Industrial organization: Theory and practice*. Oxford University Press.

Wright, B. E., & Pandey, S. K. (2011). Public organizations and mission valence: When does mission matter? *Administration & Society, 43*(1), 22–44.

Wuichet, P. A. (2000). How resources affect and stimulate collaboration. *New Directions for Philanthropic Fundraising, 2000*(28), 67–84.

Yui, M., & Gregory, R. (2018). Quakes and aftershocks: Organisational restructuring in the New Zealand state sector, 1960–2017. *Policy Quarterly, 14*(3), 25–32.

About the Authors

Rodney Scott

Rodney Scott is an Adjunct Professor at the University of New South Wales. Since 2014, he has worked for the State Services Commission and Public Service Commission in a variety of roles, including Director of Research and International Engagement, Chief Policy Advisor, and Chief Science Advisor. In 2017 he led the project to develop the Commission's Toolkit for Shared Problems. He is a member of the New Zealand Chief Science Advisors Forum, the Chair of the Victoria University of Wellington School of Government Trust, and a board member of the Institute for Public Administration of New Zealand.

Rodney completed a PhD in Public Administration from the University of Queensland, was a 2017 Innovations Fellow at Harvard University's Kennedy School of Government, a 2018 Fellow in Practice at Oxford University's Blavatnik School of Government, and is an Affiliated Researcher with Cambridge University's Bennett Institute for Public Policy. He has written extensively in books and journals on public administration, including several texts on interagency collaboration.

Eleanor Merton

Eleanor Merton is a researcher and public servant. She has worked for the Public Service Commission since 2020 in a variety of roles, including as Research Advisor and was formerly Head of Research for the McGuinness Institute, a leading non-partisan public policy think tank in New Zealand.

Eleanor has edited and published on a range of public policy and public administration issues, including interagency collaboration, the New Zealand system of government, and public sector reform.

The views and opinions expressed in this Element are the authors' own and do not represent the Public Service Commission or the New Zealand government.

Cambridge Elements ≡

Public and Nonprofit Administration

Andrew Whitford
University of Georgia
Andrew Whitford is Alexander M. Crenshaw Professor of Public Policy in the School of Public and International Affairs at the University of Georgia. His research centers on strategy and innovation in public policy and organization studies.

Robert Christensen
Brigham Young University
Robert Christensen is professor and George Romney Research Fellow in the Marriott School at Brigham Young University. His research focuses on prosocial and antisocial behaviours and attitudes in public and nonprofit organizations.

About the Series
The foundation of this series are cutting-edge contributions on emerging topics and definitive reviews of keystone topics in public and nonprofit administration, especially those that lack longer treatment in textbook or other formats. Among keystone topics of interest for scholars and practitioners of public and nonprofit administration, it covers public management, public budgeting and finance, nonprofit studies, and the interstitial space between the public and nonprofit sectors, along with theoretical and methodological contributions, including quantitative, qualitative, and mixed-methods pieces.

The Public Management Research Association
The Public Management Research Association improves public governance by advancing research on public organizations, strengthening links among interdisciplinary scholars, and furthering professional and academic opportunities in public management.

Cambridge Elements ᐀

Public and Nonprofit Administration

Elements in the Series

Printed in the United States
by Baker & Taylor Publisher Services